GETTING ACQUAINTED WITH THE BASICS OF BANK PRODUCTS

ZORAN TEMELKOV

DEDICATION

Dedicated to every person willing to get acquainted with the basics of bank products and services

CONTENTS

CHAPTER ONE:
THE DECISION WHERE TO BANK

1.1 Introduction

Because of our needs for financial products and services, banks as well as other financial institutions have become an integral part of our lives. Activities such as money transfer, payments, purchases and savings are all performed through banks or other type of financial company. Because of the significant role of banks in our lives we should strive to better understand them or more precisely to better understand their products and services. Since we make numerous decision related to bank products and services having basic knowledge about these products and services, would enable us to make better financial decision.

Our interaction with the banking sector with the need for opening a bank account. Although it may be a rather straight forward process it can be time consuming. This is imposing the need for better understanding matters associated with opening a bank account.

Sometimes in our lives for one reason or another, we may want to change our bank. Although this may be a difficult decision, the need for switching a bank may arise. The process of deciding whether or not to switch to another bank involves different steps. The decision to switch a bank should be based on couple of things. Namely, information should be gathered about the value we get from switching a bank, the process of changing current bank, and the way this process will affect our credit score.

When it comes to selecting a new bank, a decision should be made regarding the type of bank to be banking with. There are different types of banks with its own advantages and disadvantages. Thus when it comes to a type of banks, the decision is between big banks, local community banks and online banks.

1.2 Opening a bank account

Before even starting discussing what do you need to open a bank account, you need to select the right bank for you. In order to choose the right bank you need to define your preferences and needs. This is in a sense that you need to know what you are looking for from your bank and what do you expect from your bank account. Be aware that different banks have different advantages suitable for different preferences and needs. The best thing would be to make a comparison table for the banks in your area (make sure to include online banks in the table). This comparison table should be consisted of the things you would expect from your bank and the aspects you would dislike about a bank. Some basic features that should be listed when making the comparison table are shown in the table below.

Bank features comparison table

Features (preferences,	Bank A	Bank B	Bank C
General Aspects			
Minimum balance			
Minim balance fees			
ATM fees			
Monthly maintenance fee			
Other fees			
Interest rates on loans			
Interest rates on savings			
Time period you will be			
New account promotions			
Switching banks offers			
FDIC insured			
Personal aspects (preferences)			
Online banking			
Mobile banking			
Customer service			
Branch network			
ATM network			
Working hours			

Types of loans available

Loan application process

While the first part of the table should list the general aspects associated with your new bank and bank account, the second part is also important because it is considering your personal preferences. Start by listing the features in two categories, a general category and personal preference category. The general category should be consisted of all common features each and every one of us would be faced with. The personal aspects category should be consisted of features specific to your needs and preferences. When it comes to some products, such as loans, make a separate row for each loan (revolving loan i.e. credit card, personal loan, car loan, mortgage, and so on).

Make sure that you include any bank promotions available. These promotion could give you value in the short run or the long run, depending on your needs.

What do you need to open a bank account?

What you need in order to open a bank account is to decide about the type of account you are planning to use. Meaning that, after selecting the bank, you should decide on the type of account you will open. There are a couple of basic account types, these are:

- Checking account – is what you need for a day-to-day activities. This account represents the most liquid type of account. Thus, you can make frequent deposits and withdrawals of money from this type of account. You could be using this account through a debit card, checks or ATM. You should be aware that money in checking account will not be earning high interest (or maybe not earn any interest at all). Get familiar with the bank's fee for products such as overdraft, and understand how you could decrease or avoid paying these fees. Other things that could be associated with your checking account, which you should know before hand, are: maintenance fees, minimum balance fees, and minimum balance. Make sure that you are familiar with the available possibilities to avoid paying fees.
- Savings account – is less liquid form of account compared to the checking account. But due to some federal regulations, more precisely Regulation D, you are limited to six transactions per month. The savings account usually serves the purpose to put aside an emergency fund, or any other short-term savings you might have. Unlike the checking account that offers low interest or no interest at all, savings account can earn you some interest income on your money. Most often, fees associated with savings account are lower than fees associated with your checking account. But, as it was the

case with checking account, you should also get familiar with fees related to the savings account.

• Certificate of deposits – this form of account has the lowest liquidity in comparison to the checking and savings account. When opening a CD you agree that you will not be using your money for certain period of time. Namely, you can open a CD for a specific term, for instance, couple of months, a year, or more. Until the expiration of the CD term, you cannot use your funds. In case you want to withdraw money prior to the maturity date of the CD, then you would have to pay an early withdrawal penalty (fee). Because of this form of agreement, the CD is bearing higher interest rate than you would normally get with a savings account.

You should know that some banks have an accounts that have combined features from these accounts. For instance, you could open a checking account that earns interest, but you are obliged by the bank to maintain a higher balance. Before deciding on the account type, you should be aware about all offers from your bank in relation to the accounts. This way, you will ensure that you have an account with the most adequate features in accordance to your needs.

After selecting your bank and account type, what you need to open a bank account is the documentation required by the bank. Thus the next step, entails that you should prepare the needed documents required by the bank to open new account. Keep in mind that these are more or less the general requirements for opening a new account, but you should always ask the bank, because there might be some additional requirements, or differences from one bank to another. Get acquainted with account application process of your new bank, should you apply in person or you can do it online. The basic list of requirements for opening a new bank account are:

• Identification – you will need to have a valid identification document. A valid identification document is a driver's license or passport. Or a state specific ID card.

• Personal details – these serve the purpose for verifying who you are, such as, name, date of birth, phone number, present address, social security number and an email address.

• Initial deposit – if there is a need to deposits money on your new account. Some banks may ask you to make an initial deposit, so make sure that you have money with you. You could also ask the bank prior to opening the account, so you would know whether they require an initial deposit to be made or not.

You should be aware that some banks might require a credit check. If you have a problematic credit history, do not be surprised if you are rejected. This credit check is done through a ChexSystems which is a consumer reporting agency.

In summary, what do you need to open a bank account is the following: select a bank, decide on the type of account, get familiar with the account opening process, and prepare the necessary documents. Make sure you go through these steps, so you are not faced with a redundant trips back and forth to your bank.

1.3 Reasons for swiitching banks

The subject of switching banks is something that every one of us will most probably consider at some point. Whether we will do it or not depends on different factors (personal or external factor, since, there are switching barriers that could force us to stay with the current bank). Regardless of the barriers, we should try to answer the question – Why switch banks? What are the reasons that could lead toward the desire or plans to change your current bank? Reasons could be found in the changes in our current life situation, dissatisfaction with our bank, competitors' products and services, and/or follow the crowd mentality (desire).

Some general reasons for switching banks are:

Life situation – one category of reasons that could lead toward the need for switching banks is the category of life situation. More precisely, changes in your life situation. There are three basic changes that could occur in your life.

- Changing the place of residence – is a common reason for switching banks for many people. There is nothing wrong with this being the reason for switching banks. But if you relocate often, then maybe you should choose to switch to a bank with widespread branch network, or a big bank having offices in different countries and cities.
- Changes in marital status – is a reason that speaks for itself. Depending on your marital status you are looking for bank accordingly. Meaning that you would be looking for products offering joint accounts or you would like to close your joint accounts and open a new (separate) personal account.
- Changes in jobs or job status – starting a new job or losing your current job could also be a reason for switching banks. Again, you are adapting your banking activities in accordance to your current living situation.

Dissatisfied with existing bank – another category of reasons that could augment your desire to change your bank is related directly to your current bank. Stated differently, you might want to change your bank, because of some general dissatisfaction with the bank or some of its products and services. Most common reasons in this category are:

- Fees – they should not be neglected in your banking activities. Thus, recognizing the importance of bank fees, people might change banks because of increase in fee level or introduction of new fees. On monthly, and especially, yearly level, fees could add up to a substantial amount, and if you are using multiple products, they can be even higher. Thus, fees can be pointed out as a separate reason that could led toward the need for switching your account (and all other products you are using) to another bank. Always be familiar with the fees you are paying for your bank products. Make periodical control for possible changes in the fees you are charged with.

- Hidden fees – this is closely related with the above reason that could stimulate you to switch banks. While, the above reason is taking into account the direct fees that you could be charged with, people also want to change banks because they are annoyed by the existence of hidden fees. This is in a sense that, the bank did not inform you about all fees that you are going to get charged with, or you are charged with additional fees for performing some activity with your bank.

- Inconvenient location – for whatever reason you have selected the specific bank, but you realize that the location of your bank is becoming inconvenient for you. Thus you want to switch to a bank that has a location in accordance to your needs. The location could be perceived in terms of the ATM network, or branch network, or even online availability.

- Decrease in interest rates on savings – initially you might be attracted by the banks' interest rate, offered on saving products. What will you do if this value is diminished? What will you do if the bank lowers the interest rate paid on your savings? For many, the answer is simple, shop around for higher interest rates and switch to the banks that will offer highest value. Although in the short run this might seem as a negligible reason to switch banks, in the long run you could be losing significant interest income, especially if you take into consideration the compounding effect.

- Increase in interest rates on mortgage – this is the opposite of the previous. While the previous reason is taking into consideration a possible decrease in interest income, this is dealing with the possibility for increase in your installment. Sudden increase in the interest rate (or APR) you pay on your mortgage or other long term loan, could hurt your financial health in the future. Thus, make sure that you keep yourself informed about the level of interest rates, especially if you have a mortgage with adjustable rate. Here you should consider two things before deciding to change your bank on the basis of this reason. First, you should examine whether there is a general trend in interest rate increase, due to changes of economic situation. Second, confirm or reject the first by analyzing whether the increase is specific to your bank only or other banks are doing it as well.

• Complicated procedures and high level of bureaucracy – while all banks require the same basic documents for opening an account or applying for loan, there could be difference between banks in the additional documents or procedures they have. You should know that, each bank has its own internal procedures and policy when it comes to different products and services. There is a certain level of unified procedures in accordance to the legal framework, but, there are also banks specific procedures. This means, that some banks may have more complicated procedures than others. Because we all want to make our lives easier, we are trying to avoid any time consuming procedures and bureaucracy. Thus, people do change to another bank instead of dealing with high level of bureaucracy and complicated procedures.

Competitors' products and services – the third category that could provide answer to the question – Why switch banks, is taking into consideration the competition. Namely, for one reason or another, the competitors have better products and services. Thus, abandoning your current bank, and choosing a competitors' bank could provide benefits for your financial health.

• Better products and services with other banks – meaning that you are planning to switch your bank because its competitors are offering more attractive products. The attractiveness of the products could be numerous. For instance, other banks may offer lower APR on loans or lower fees. They might have faster or easier loan application process. You might find that other banks have better customer service, or better ATM or branch network. In addition, maybe you want to conduct your financial activities online, thus you could switch to a technologically advanced bank.

• Promotional offers – as funny it may seems, using the benefits from promotional offers made by competitors could also be a reason for some people to switch banks. It may be funny to switch banks solely to grasp a cash bonus. But if you have higher value after switching, then people could do the switch. Be careful when switching banks on the basis of promotional offers. You need to understand the value of these promotional offers, and their impact on your financial health.

Follow the crowd – could be also explained as a word of mouth reason for changing your bank. This is in a sense that some other bank has been recommended to you by a friend or relative. Your desire to switch to a bank suggested by someone close to you, is driven by their experience they have had with the new bank. In addition, your business partner could recommend you a bank where you could switch in order to ease the process of doing business. If this is the reason you are considering to change your bank, and open an account with other bank, then think twice. Don't rush into things just to follow the crowd. You should evaluate the services and products of the recommended bank, in terms of their fit for you financial habits. Gather information about all relevant services and products you are using, and might be using in the future, and make comparison with the products and services offered to you by your current bank.

Think for a moment – Why switch banks? Do you know the reason that caused you to switch banks, have you ever thought to change your current bank? There are different reasons that could lead to the desire to switch to another bank. Whether you will do the switch is an entirely different issue. But, if you could find a better terms and could have high benefits if you switch to another bank, then you should do it.

1.4 Going through the hassle of switching banks – Is It Worth It?

Customers are changing their favorite brands when they feel disappointed or when another brand is offering higher satisfaction. Thus the pursuit for higher satisfaction is resulting in customers seeking new products and/or new companies. This possibility is offered by the fact that there is not much of a hassle involved in switching between physical products. Consider what you did when you wanted to change your favorite chocolate, or juice, or whatever else that you have changed. Was it time-consuming? Did it cost you anything? Did you have problems finding another product that is similar or even better? Hopefully the answer to all these questions is "No". Now ask yourself – why don't you switch to another bank? Are you really satisfied with your bank? Unlike physical products, switching banks has been a time-consuming process until couple of years ago. Not many people were eager to go through the entire process of changing banks, regardless of their possible dissatisfaction with their banks. For this reasons some banks became a "customer lazy" banks. Meaning that they were focused on attracting new customers, and forgetting about the existing clients.

Nowadays, the technological innovation, increase in awareness of customers regarding their needs, changing customer preferences, as well as the increased competition in banking industry, has changed the process of switching banks. Meaning that it is much easier to change your bank today, and most likely it will become even easier in the future. The constant pursuit for new clients has resulted in banks offering to cover the process of switching banks for you. An additional benefit is that many banks offer some kind of reward (cash reward) in case you switch banks i.e. transfer your paycheck and savings to their bank.

What comes next is to ask – if it is worth switching banks? A single unified answer could not be provided to this question. The reason is that each and every one of us has different perception about the adequacy of his/her bank in relation to his/her needs. Consider for example the need of your grandparents, your parents and your needs (or your children needs). Is there any difference, most probably, one would like to have bank offering technological solutions, another would look for low fees, or face to face communication etc.

Things to consider before switching banks

Although a unified answer could not be provided, there are some general issues that should be considered before changing banks, or from time to time to see if you should switch to another bank. You should consider the following:

- The fees you are paying for the services – you should always compare the fees of your bank with fees of other banks. Don't think about these fees as a small amount, because they could be a substantial amount on a yearly base.
- Consider the interest rates you are paying on the overdraft as well as loans. Go through the interest rates charged by other banks periodically. Maybe you could find a cheaper loan to refinance your existing debt, thus saving on the interest rate charge.
- Consider the interest rates you are receiving on your savings account – a small percentage difference could mean substantial difference in your overall savings amount in the long run.
- Technologically proactive bank – look at the technological solutions and services of your bank in relation to those offered by other banks. Is your bank keeping the pace with new technology? Is your bank offering the newest technological services (mobile banking, online payments, online application, etc.)?
- Customer service – is your bank offering and adequate customer service? Are you able to resolve any possible disputes in short time? This is the part that many clients do not consider an important. The truth when a problem appears with some transaction, usually it is the most important transaction (Murphy's Law), thus it will require a solution as fast as possible.

Taking into consideration the above issues, should serve you as a decent base to help you decide if switching banks is worth the effort. But keep in mind that you should not switch banks very often, because it might signal lack of stability in your behavior.

1.5 Short run and long run value of bank switching offers

The last financial crises has increased the customer awareness and nowadays, customers are demanding more for less. In an era of rapid technological development, increased customer awareness and change in customers' preferences, some banks see an opportunity to increase their customer base. Banks are trying to utilize this trend of bank clients demanding more value for less money. Banks have increased the value of their bank switching offers, bonuses and rewards to make people open an account with them, and later on use some of bank's products and services.

These bank switching offers or new checking account bonuses and rewards are affecting the decision of a potential client. While in the past bank switching offers entailed some small home appliances (for instance a toaster), nowadays these offers could be in the form of cash, cash back, removal of fees, lower interest rates, story credits, etc. Thus making the offers more interesting than ever. They are especially interesting because some of them give short-term value while other provide value for you in the long run.

Although these offers are interesting and valuable they can complicate your decision-making process when selecting your new bank on the basis of the offers. For this reason before making a decision and analyzing the offers you should define whether you are switching banks often or you will work with the new bank in the long run.

Things to consider when choosing a bank switching offers

As it was mentioned, before deciding on the best bank switching offer, you should be aware about your personal bank switching habits. Namely, you should know whether you are switching banks often or you have more stable behavior when it comes to your bank. Identifying your bank switching pattern will provide you with the information of whether to go for a short-term offer or long-term offer. Knowing the type of value you want will make your decision easier. This in a sense that you could immediately exclude some of the offers for switching bank accounts. But in order to be able to exclude some of the offers, you must primarily rank them. When preparing the list of bank offers, rank these offers in two categories: short-term offer and long-term offers. That way you will know which list to eliminate, and you will be left with the list that provides the highest value.

Let's consider a short run value offer. The most common short-term value offer would be the cash offer. This is not to imply that the amount of cash offered is small. The idea is to point out that cash offer for switching account is a onetime offer. Consequently, after the cash is deposited to your account, the value is gone (especially after you spend it). That is why this offer is offering value in the short. In case you do not plan to change your bank anytime soon, then you do not have any additional benefits for selecting the specific bank.

On the other hand, offers with long-term value could be more beneficial to you. These offers will provide benefits during the entire time you are with the selected bank. Considered the effect if the offer includes a waiving of certain fees if you switch your current account. Some fees can be substantial on a yearly level. What about the effect from an offer for lower interest rates on loans or higher interest rates on saving accounts? What is the value of a cash back rewards, is it short-term or long-term value? The aforementioned examples offer much more value in the long run, although at first it seems that it is better to go for the cash bonus. If you are planning to stay with your bank for many years to come, then it is better to switch to a bank where the offer include benefits for: fees, interest rate, or cash back possibilities.

Imagine that you switch your current account and transfer all you savings with the new bank. One time cash offer will be interesting, but if you stay with the new bank for many years it might turn out to be a bad decision. For example, imagine you have $10,000.00 in your saving account. Now you should decide between two offers, a $100 cash offer or additional 0.5% interest on your savings. What will you choose if you plan to be with the new bank for couple of years? Most likely someone will go for the cash money. Very bad decision. Calculate the additional interest income you will receive if you have selected the interest rate on saving account bank switching offer. It turns out that at the end of the first year you would receive additional $50, and you plan to stay with your bank for couple of years. Imagine that each year you save additional $5,000.00 of your yearly income. Then the second year you will have $15,000.00 on your saving account. Thus, the second year you will take extra $75 in interest income. This is the reason that you should always select the offer that is offering the highest value in the long run. You could make similar calculation with the fees you are paying. If there is an offer that will remove some fees, how much money will you save in the long run? Considered the money you would save if you go for a cash back on purchases offer.

When selecting a bank switching offer, the first step is to decide how long you will be a client of the new bank. The second step involves categorization of available bank switching offers according to their short-term value or long-term value. If you plan to be a short period of time with your new bank, then you could go for the cash offer. But if you plan to stay longer period with your new bank then the cash is not an option. You should choose an offer that gives you most value in the long run (whether it will be a fee waiver, increase in interest rate on saving account, cash back on you purchases), don't go for the cash immediately. Decide wisely before switching banks.

1.6 How to switch banks ?

When dissatisfied with your current bank, you might (or must) start considering the possibility to switch banks. Reasons because of which you would switch banks are numerous, but the aim here is to briefly describe some basic steps in the process of how to switch banks. When you are ready to change bank you have a couple of alternatives (bank wise): large bank, local bank or online bank. You could also consider switching to a credit union. Coming back to the banks as an alternative, the decision about the type of bank you want to switch to is entirely up to you. As far as the process for switching banks, there are a couple of basic steps that you should consider.

Basics steps in the process of changing banks

There are some basic activities that you should perform before switching banks. These activities should help you to painlessly switch banks, and limit your additional charges and/or fees that might appear.

- Decide on your new bank – your primary step should be to decide which bank will be your new bank. Although, you might read a recommendation that this should be a second or third step, this should be your primary action. This is so because, you should start the bank switching process before you close down your account with the old bank. In addition, knowing beforehand which bank you are going to, will help you speed up the process of switching banks. Moreover, having decided on your new bank, will prove beneficial for reducing the hassle that could be involved during the process of switching banks.

- Prepare your documents – in order for you to open an account with another bank you should fulfill a couple of requirements. For the purpose of assuring smooth opening of your new account, make sure that you have gathered all the necessary documents. This way you could save redundant trips to your bank, and open the account faster. Thus, before opening your new account, remember that you need to make sure to know what do you need to open a bank account.

- Don't use your existing bank to make any payments or transactions – Plan ahead and withdraw enough cash to last during the entire process of changing banks. When withdrawing cash, aside of the cash you need for your everyday purchases, you should also consider the amount you will need to open a new account. Do not use checks, or debit cards issued from your old bank anymore. Before closing existing accounts, make sure that you have decided on your new bank. Never make any anger driven decision about your current bank. Meaning that you should not close your existing account immediately after someone in your old bank has pissed you off. Prior to changing banks, you should consider whether you really need to change your bank.

• Set up your automatic transactions – after opening your new account, and stopped using your old account, you should consider your automatic transactions. Meaning that, now is the time you should switch your direct deposits (redirect your income) and bill pay. Stated differently, when opening new account with different bank, do not forget that you should also make switch to the following: direct deposits from paychecks, unemployment benefits, different bill payments, linked accounts, smart phone apps, pension and/or annuity income, income from investments, etc. Basically, you should consider switching to your new bank (thus, canceling with your old bank) all the activities you have. To make sure you have set up all of your transactions with your new bank, make a check list. Meaning that, you should make a list of all of your transactions and apps linked to your old bank.

• Transfer the majority of your money to your new account – do not transfer all of your money into the new account. Make sure that you have a certain balance left on your old account before closing it. This is especially important if you do not have the habit to keep a clear record of your transactions and checks or purchases. Although you may see a recommendation to transfer all your money to the new account, a wise thing would be something else. Namely, to protect yourself against some additional charges that may come from your old bank. You should maintain some minimum balance on your account in case you have forgotten checks or some forgotten transaction. Keep both accounts active for about three months (maybe more if you are not sure about the number of forgotten checks or transactions). In addition, pay attention to the minimum balance required on your account with your old bank, so as to avoid minimum balance fees. If you transfer all of your money to the new bank, some checks might bounce. This could result in you paying a late-payment fees on your old account. Make sure you have enough balance on your old account to clear any forgotten checks and transactions and avoid paying minimum balance fees or late-payment fees.

In order to make the switching banks process easier for clients, banks are offering so-called "Switch kit". This switch kit should guide you step by step through the process of switching banks. The switch kit could ease your process of switching banks. You could ask your new bank whether they offer a switch kit when opening new account for the purpose of changing banks.

Switching banks is an important decision that should be made carefully. You should never decide to switch banks in a moment of anger. If you have decided to switch banks, the next thing is to gather information regarding the question – How to switch banks? More or less the process of switching banks in USA is same between banks. But the steps performed on your behalf could be different from person to person. Some want to close down the old bank account before opening new account, others would maintain both account simultaneously. Generally speaking, there is no right or wrong thinking. But, as an informational guide, when asking yourself how to switch banks, you should: select your new bank, open an account, stop using your old account, have enough money to go through the transfer period, automate your transactions with your new account, and don't close the old account for couple of months.

1.7 The effect of changing banks on you credit score

One common belief is that switching a bank account will negatively affect your credit score. This is both, true and false at the same time. The effect from closing a bank account on your credit score may or may not be negative. It may not affect your credit score because you should understand that it is not a credit card. But on the other hand your credit score could be affected when applying for overdraft. Moreover, when opening a bank account, your new bank could perform a credit check. This credit check could have some negative effect on your credit score (if the bank performs a hard inquiry). For that reason, you should primarily understand what are: soft inquiry and hard inquiry, and how they can affect your credit score.

In its very basic, a **soft inquiry** is generated by a credit pull not related to any line of credit. This form of inquiry could be performed by you if you want to check your credit score or when your employer is making a background check on you. In addition, the soft inquiry can also be performed when opening a bank account. You should be aware that soft inquiry can be performed without your permission. Whatever the reason for soft inquiry, you should know that this inquiry does not affect your credit score. Noteworthy mentioning is the fact that although soft inquiry doesn't have negative effect on your credit score, it does show up on your credit report.

Unlike soft inquiry, the **hard inquiry** is generated when you want to apply for a loan. This type of inquiry can have negative effect on your credit score. Thus, the hard inquiry could decrease your credit score by up to five points. Although it is not a common practice for banks to perform a hard inquiry, when you open a bank account, you could be a subject to this type of inquiry. Meaning that the bank could perform hard inquiry on your credit report. This hard inquiry will be recorded as credit inquiry on your credit report, even though it is performed when you open an account and not applying for a loan. The good thing with hard inquiries is that you should give a permission. In case a hard inquiry has been performed for you without your consent, you can dispute the report.

When closing an account it will not have any impact on your credit score, because the account is not a line of credit. Keep in mind though that changing banks doesn't have any significant impact on your credit score, unless you failed to fulfill your part of the account agreement. Any behavior which is not in accordance to the account agreement could be recorded in the consumer report i.e. the ChexSystmes report. Since, this report is taking into consideration only the activity with your accounts, it does not affect your credit score.

Inform yourself about the type of inquiry your potentially new bank will perform, so you would know whether changing banks will affect your credit score. Make sure that you know whether they will make a soft inquiry or a hard inquiry. This way you will know whether there would be a decrease in your credit score or not. Keep in mind that when opening new account, most probably you will be a subject to a soft inquiry. Thus, you have nothing to worry about, because this form of inquiry does not affect your credit score. On the other hand, some banks may perform a hard inquiry, for which they need your permission. This form of inquiry has negative effect on your credit score (it can knock down up to 5 points).

1.8 Reasons why you should use online banking

New technology had major impact on the way we perform our everyday activities. The way we communicate, the way we make purchases has change drastically during the last decade. Of course the way we bank has also changed with the development of online banking.

While the influence of the technology is criticized by some, the reality is that it has made our lives easier. This is especially true for online banking. Although brick-and-mortar banking has its own advantages, there are numerous reasons to use online banking.

Before you read some reasons as to why you should be banking online, think about the things you don't like with the brick-and-mortar banking.

Some prevailing reasons which could help you decide to bank online are listed below.

Instant access to your accounts – know your balances at any time

In the past you have been waiting for the next business day to check your bank statements or to see your available balance. In addition to this waiting period, you must go to the physical location of the bank. Nowadays, this time-consuming task is eliminated when using online banking. Not only you have access to your accounts 24/7, online banking also eliminates the need for going to your branch.

Keep track of your transactions

The need for better control over our transactions should be pointed out as separate reason for banking online. Specifically, with online banking you can keep track of your transactions 24/7. You have overview of all cleared transaction, pending transactions as well as transaction you have made in the past. You are able to see your balance at any given moment, simply by going to your online banking page.

Deposit your checks with your mobile device

Because of the technological advancements, some banks offer the option to deposit checks through online banking, as long as your mobile device is equipped with camera.

Faster transfer of funds

Instead of going to the bank when you want to transfer money from one account to another, you can perform this process online.

Option to pay your bills

Not only you can transfer funds between accounts, banking online also enables you to pay your bills online. Thus, you can eliminate the time consuming activities associated with physical payment of your bills. For instance, you can avoid the need for stamps. Furthermore, with online banking you are eliminating the risk of lost check. Also, you can create an automatic payment for your bills.

Better manage your money by connecting online banking with personal finance apps

Banking online offers an option to connect your mobile banking with personal finance apps. This is easing the process of keeping track of your finances and budgeting decisions as well as spending habits.

Make savings when using online making

When using your online banking for your banking activities and payments you can save money in couple of ways. First, banks could charge lower fee when using online banking for transfer of funds and/or paying bills. Second, eliminating the need for stamps could also save your money. Third, eliminating the need to visit your local bank could save you money on gas.

In a fast-paced environment we all strive to get as much spare time as we can. Thus, in a time constrained environment the traditional way of banking could impact our stress free time. Fortunately online banking is available. Not only banking online is enabling us to save certain amount of money but it offers something more valuable. Online banking offers the possibility to limit the time consuming activities such as: going to your bank or waiting in line at your bank. Although some generations are resisting the usage of online banking, they are beginning to understand the benefits from it and use it accordingly.

1.9 Reasons to bank with big banks

A notable trend during the last couple of years is the change in customer preferences towards big banks. Namely, customers are starting to bank with smaller banks or local community banks. Because they choose not to bank with big banks they are taking their money away from the big national banks. This trend is evident in the period after the last financial crisis.

But the questions is whether this is a smart move or not. Should customers bank with big banks or transfer their money into local community bank? What are some of the reasons to bank with big banks?

Banking with big banks offer certain advantages over the smaller community banks. Some of the reasons to select a big bank are listed below.
Developed ATM network

It is obvious that because of the scale of operation of big banks they have better developed network of ATM and branches as well. You can find an ATM of some big bank all over the country. The difference in number of ATM's and geographical coverage is obvious. You can use an ATM of a big bank all over the nation, while this is not the case with a local community bank.
Developed branch network

Another reason to bank with big banks aside of the ATM network is their network of branches. Big banks have well established network of branches in which they offer their products and services. The difference is more than evident if we compare for instance the number of branches of Bank of America and Oak Valley Community Bank. According to the information regarding the number of branches Bank of America branch network is composed of 4639 branches while Oak Valley Banks has 17 branches.
Implementation of latest technology

Big banks have resources and strategy to follow the latest technology. The sheer size of big banks and the level of resources they have enables them to digitize their services. Local community banks most often have limited amount of resources and limited size of customer base (locally). Meaning that investments in costly technological solutions may not be justified. Therefore you are not enjoying the benefits of technological advancements with local banks. It should be noted though, that this should not be taken for granted. There are some smaller banks who have been following the technological developments.

Diversity in product offerings (wide assortment of financial products and services)

When banking with big banks you have a better chance of finding adequate financial product or service. Because of the scale of operations and the number of customers, big banks are able to create versatile product offerings. Unlike local community banks, it is profitable for banks to develop different types of products. Local banks on the other hand may not be able to offer specific products or custom products . Smaller banks have limited demand for these products because their customer base is smaller.

There are many reasons to be banking with big banks. You should choose the type of bank in accordance to your personal preferences for financial products and services. In addition, don't forget to take into account your life style before you decide on the type of bank. This is in a sense that if you are a regular traveler it may be a smart move to go with the big banks because of their geographical coverage. Moreover, if you move often then banking with a local bank will mean that you have to switch banks each time you move to a new location.

1.10 Bank switching offers

Bank switching offers could be in the form of cash bonus, cash back opportunity, air miles, story credits, higher APR, fee waiving, or even a bonus for referring a friend. Bank switching offers could usually be in the form of a new bank account promotions, new bank account bonuses, etc. Whatever name we call them, at the end their primary goal is to persuade you to change your bank, and open a new account with another bank.

As it has been mentioned, the reward you will earn for opening a new account (checking or savings account) can vary from bank to bank. Before deciding on the bank you will open your new account with, make sure that you have gathered information and you understand the attractiveness of each switching incentive. Noteworthy mentioning is that most of these bank switching incentives have an expiration date. Meaning that they are valid for a specific period, or during a specific session.

Choosing the bank switching offer should be in accordance to your habits and preferences. Thus, if you have a habit to increase your savings and/or direct deposits then you should look for a bonus such as the one offered by Capital One. Namely, Capital One is offering a fee free savings account, and the possibility to earn up to $500 bonus. To qualify for the bonus, you should deposit the qualifying amount in accordance to the terms, within the first 10 days of opening your account. In addition, you should maintain the required balance for 90 days, after the 10 days period.

The so-called balance/bonus tiers (offers) include: $50 bonus if you deposit $5,000, $100 bonus for a $10,000 deposit, with $20,000 you are entitled to a $200 bonus, $400 bonus when you deposit $40,000 and a maximum of $500 bonus for a $50,000 deposit.

BMO Harris offers a $200 cash bonus when you open a checking account (or the switch to a BMO Harris checking account bonus). Santander bank will give you $150 bonus within 30 days after you open an eligible checking account. The conditions to receive the bonus are: to have a direct deposits of at least $500 within the first 90 days and your account should be opened for 90 days. In addition, you could waive the fee with the Simply right checking with Santander bank. Meaning that, you could avoid the $10 monthly fee if you make one transaction (a deposits, transfer, withdrawal) during the month.

SunTrust – is offering two possibilities. The first one is a checking bonus of up to $200 if you open a new Sun Trust checking account with direct deposit (applicable only for new clients). In order to be eligible for the bonus, you need to make, at least, $2000 in direct deposits within the first 60 days. You are eligible for a $100 checking bonus if you open an Essential checking account with a minimum of $500 in direct deposits within 60 days.

Christian Community Credit Union – will give you a $100 bonus if you decide to open a free checking account with them. If you go for the free checking you are also entitled to receive additional benefits. Some of these benefits are: no monthly service fee, no minimum balance required, and free mobile banking.

Northpointe Bank is attracting new customers, through the usage of an appealing APR and fee waiver. Meaning that, Northpointe Bank will pay you a 5% APR for a balances of up to $5,000. Moreover, you could get a refund of up to $10 a month for ATM fees, and $3 a month for person to person payment fees.

With the Citigold relationship program you have the opportunity to earn a $500 cash bonus. To be entitled to a bonus, first, you need to open a new consumer checking account. Second, you should make an eligible deposit equal to, or in excess of $50,000, with the first 30 days of opening the account. You will receive the bonus if you maintain a minimum of $50,000 balance the next 30 days.

Bank of America is offering the possibility for a new client to earn up to $150 bonus. The bonus is consisted of two components. The first one, that could earn you a $100 bonus, is related to a checking or savings account. Namely, to qualify for this bonus, you should open a Bank of America Core Checking or Bank of America Interest Checking account. After opening any of the account, you should set up and receive 2 eligible direct deposits of minimum $250 each, within the first 90 days of opening your account. The second component is related to your tax refund. You have the opportunity to earn additional $50 bonus if you direct deposit your federal tax return of a minimum of $500 into any of the Bank of America checking or savings account.

Aside of the cash bonuses and cash back rewards, there is also another interesting offer made by the banks. Namely, they offer a possibility for their clients to earn additional bonus by referring their friends or families. These offers are interesting because, not only you take a bonus for opening a new account, but also, you take a bonus if someone you have referred to the bank opens a new account.

If you have a large circle of people you know who are dissatisfied with their bank, or are simply looking to switch to another bank, the referral bonus offered by some banks could provide high value, and this is to say cash value for you. These offers should be of particular interest for students when they are at the early stage of the need to use bank products and services.

HSBC is offering a bonus when you refer a friend. If you refer a friend who opens a qualifying HSBC premier or advanced checking account, you will receive a $100. The catch is that the friend referring reward is limited to $1,000 per calendar year. Of course there are requirements that should be fulfilled. Standford Federal Credit Union is trying to attract the students by offering a $25 per student referred. Each (you and your friend) one will receive a $25.

Wings Financial Credit Union offer up to $500 reward per year for referring a friend or family member, through the program called ReferLive. The referred friend or family member should open a Wings First Class Checking Account set up e-statements, and has a direct deposit of minimum $300. Afterwards, you and the person you referred will each receive a $50 Visa reward card.

Banks in USA have a wide spectrum of offers and incentives for opening new checking or saving account with them. One of the factors that should be taken into consideration when deciding whether to switch banks or not, are the bank switching offers. You should not neglect these rewards because they could be beneficial for you in the long run, or at least the short run, by doing something you would do anyway, open a new bank account. Thus, look for the banks with switching offers that will be in accordance to your needs and preferences. But, when deciding about your new bank, you should not base your decision solely on the offers for switching banks, there are many other factors that should be taken into consideration.

Coming back to the bank switching offers, what kind of bonus or reward will make you open an account with a specific bank? Do these banks switching offers provide any value for you? Are they attractive?

1.11 Conclusion

The purpose of this chapter was to present the basics related to the decision of choosing the right bank. You might need to choose a bank if you are banking for the first time or if you want to change your current bank. There are numerous aspects that should be taken into account when selecting the right bank.

Before choosing a bank and opening an account, there are two things that should be considered. The first one is that we should select a bank on the basis of our needs and life style. Second, we should go through the different types of accounts and see which account will be in accordance to the needs and preferences.

Noteworthy mentioning is that cash offers for opening an account or changing a bank are not always the best rewards. All types of rewards should be considered and measured against your needs in the future. While cash on hand may seems to be attractive today, fee waivers or cash back could be worth in the future. Cash on hand is a one-time deal, cash back or fee waiver could be enjoyed each year.

CHAPTER TWO:
CREDIT CARDS BASICS

2.1 Introduction

While chapter one had the objective to present the basic issues affecting your decision to choose a bank, this chapter is intended to provide an overview about the basic issues related to one of the most used financial product offered by banks i.e. the credit cards.

Credit cards are financial product used on regular basis. Thus, adequate understanding of what they represent and how they work is a must when it comes to appropriate management of credit card debt and personal finances in general. Having a credit card(s) can provide benefits but it can also lead toward increase debt levels. For this reason, the starting point should be to consider the real need of owning one or more credit cards.

When it comes to understanding how they work it is important to get acquainted with the different types of credit cards offered by banks. Moreover, getting familiar with the cost of credit card is of utmost importance. Acquiring knowledge about credit card APR will be beneficial for understanding the cost of using credit card in different manners and for different purposes.

The last step when it comes to credit cards is to decide on the most appropriate credit cards according to your needs and life style as well as to decide whether you need to have one or more credit cards.

2.2 Considering the real need for credit card(s)

Before you continue reading, keep in mind that the need to have a credit card is explained having in mind that you are a financial responsible person. Meaning that you do not have the urge to spend money on unnecessary things, and make purchases of items you do not really need. Having a credit card could be considered a double-edged sword. This is in a sense that it can be beneficial for you, but on the other side it could drag you down even more in debt. You could end up paying high interest rate on your credit card debt and the possibility to be caught by the vicious repayment circle if you have (most probably you will have) more than one credit card. Thus, you should be careful when considering whether or not you need a credit card.

Having a credit card could be a very useful tool for your everyday life, as long as it is used correctly. The need for credit card is imposing the need to go through the ways that it could make your life easier. In addition, some issues are justifying the need for owning a credit card. Let's look at some issues that should be taken into consideration when deciding whether you need a credit card or not.

Credit card offers security – minimizing the need for cash

When having a credit card, you do not need to have large amount of cash with you which is increasing your safety. Imagine you have a plan to purchase a more expensive item. Not having a credit card will force you to carry hundreds or thousands of dollars with you in cash. There is a possibility for couple of scenarios to happen. The first scenario is you go and make the purchase. Great. The second and third scenarios are not so great. Walking around with cash in your pockets could result in losing your money, your cash could fall out of your pockets, or you could forget your handbag or purse somewhere. The third scenario is that you could end up being mugged, if an immoral person notice that you carry a substantial amount of cash. Having a credit card with you could increase your safety because you will not be a target of criminal activities of a person desiring fast cash. Even if you got mugged or lose your wallet (purse) or whatever, then you simply call the bank and the credit card is no longer valid. This is limiting your loss, which is highly important in times when every penny counts. In addition, if your credit card is stolen and used for (unauthorized) purchases, there is a possibility that the bank will reimburse certain portion (in some cases the entire amount) of the loss. According to the Federal Trade Commission your liability for unauthorized charges is up to $50. Meaning that you limit your maximum loss to $50 (off course there are certain conditions when this does not apply).

Need a credit card when travelling

Another issue that should be considered when deciding on whether or not you need a credit card, is the traveling. Imagine traveling to other country, not having a credit card means that you need to carry cash with you. The amount of cash you will have with you should be enough to last for the entire trip. How much money you need to have on hand to pay for accommodation, evenings out, food and beverage, or car rental services?

Moreover, having a credit card means that you do not need to worry about the currency. When traveling abroad you should be aware about the currency and the need to exchange your country's currency for the local currency. This is not a complex process but it could be a time-consuming process if you can't find an exchange bureau near you or the exchange bureau is closed. The credit card is eliminating the need for you to convert your money in the money of the country you are going to. You could pay with your credit card and the conversion from one currency to another is performed automatically (keep in mind though, that in some cases there is unfavorable exchange rate).

Moreover, nowadays, it is difficult to make any hotel reservations without a credit card. In cases where you could make a reservation without a credit card, you should bank wire the funds to the hotel (or send a check) in order to make a reservation. This could be a time-consuming task, and also an expensive task due to the fees.

The need to have cash for every day purchases

Owning a credit card could also be beneficial for your everyday purchases. Meaning that there is no need to be constantly worried whether you have cash with you or not. Not owning a credit card, means that before going to the store you must first go to the bank and make a withdrawal so that you could pay for your supplies. In addition, you spend your cash, and again, you must run to the bank to withdraw additional cash to make a purchase. The credit card is eliminating the need to withdraw money, at least money for the purchases. You could go and make the purchase whenever you want, without the need to run to the bank and make withdrawals.

Possibility to utilize any additional benefits and rewards

Banks and other institutions offer numerous rewards when taking and/or using a credit card. Thus, not having a credit card is excluding you from the possibility to enjoy these benefits. These rewards and benefits could be different, depending on the issuer of the credit card. The most common rewards include: cash-back on your purchases (groceries, gasoline, etc.), airline miles, gas points, discounts, access to concert, VIP treatment, and much more.

Credit card as an emergency fund

If, for whatever reason, you are in a situation when you do not have an emergency fund, owning a credit card could offer some safety. Not having a credit card and/or an emergency fund in situation when an unexpected expense has occurred could leave you in a troubled position. This is in a sense that you could not swiftly cover the unforeseen expense. Then you need to borrow money from your parents, friends and family in general, letting them know that you have a financial problem. For this reason, having a credit card could be a valuable alternative, serving as an emergency fund, at least until you accumulate enough capital to have real emergency fund. This could be a good reason as to why you need a credit card.

Having your own expense tracking system

Keeping a track record of your purchases on a monthly base is highly important and also a time-consuming task. It is important because that way you could maintain control over your budget as well as spending level. It is time-consuming because you have to record every purchase you have made throughout the month. Having a credit card helps you tracking your expenses hassle free. It could be said that a credit card, can in some way, serve as your accountant (LOL) because it will keep record of all your transactions for you.

Building your credit score through payment history

Having a good credit score is extremely valuable and important when you decide to take on a mortgage or any other form of loan. This is in terms of the easiness for getting approved as well as the interest rate you will pay (the higher the credit score, the lower the interest rate should be). The credit score is calculated on the basis of couple of elements, each having its own weight in the overall score. When calculating your FICO score, noteworthy mentioning is that payment history determines 35% of your FICO score.

Having a credit card, means that you are building up a credit history, which will prove to be beneficial in the future. The positive impact on your credit score will be evident if you use your credit card wisely, you should always pay your monthly minimum on outstanding amount. Stated differently you should set in place a good managing practices with your card. This is positive because bank lenders will have track records about your financial behavior. Meaning that you will help in their decision-making process since they can examine your habits and awareness in repayment of your outstanding amount. If you don't have credit card (or other loans) then you could be placed in the category of borrower with low credit score (remember, payment history accounts for 35% of the FICO score).

As with everything else, the final decision regarding the question whether you need a credit card or not, is entirely yours. But, before making any decision, you should be aware about the benefits you could have when owning a credit card. Also, you should consider the effect on your everyday activities. This is in a sense that having a credit card could significantly reduce the time you spend on performing important but time-consuming activities.

2.3 How credit cards work?

Credit cards have become a must have in our everyday life. Their usage has increased continually since they were first introduced. Most probably you have at least one in your wallet, or you are planning to apply for one. There are numerous reasons that support the need for a credit cards. Thus, you should understand how credit cards work. Although they are useful financial product, if not used properly, they could jeopardize your financial health. You could end up with a pile of debt, and worsen finances. Thus, knowing how credit cards work, could help you better manage your credit card debt.

What is a credit card?

A credit card is a product offered by banks and other financial institutions. A credit card can be viewed as line of credit (revolving credit), or short-term loan. You are basically borrowing money every time you use the credit card to make a purchase (there are other ways to use it as well). The approved line of credit is the maximum amount of funds you can use as you desire. Thus, credit cards provide an easy way to borrow money for a short period of time. In its physical form, credit card is a plastic card. You can use your credit card to pay for different goods or services, or withdraw cash from ATM. Keep in mind that when using your credit card you have the obligation to make the minimum payment on your balance defined by the issuer.

Difference between a credit card and a debit card

Before proceeding to the explanation of how credit cards work, there is a need to briefly explain the difference between credit and debit card. Because they are physically same, some people confuse one with the other. From the aforementioned, it is obvious that a credit card is a form of a loan. Every time you use your credit card to pay for something or make a cash advance at the ATM, you are basically borrowing money. You are obliged to repay these money at a later date, in accordance to the credit card agreement. Of course, you could be charged an interest for the balance used.

On the other hand, debit cards can be used in the same manner as the credit cards, but the difference is that you do not have the repayment obligation. This is so because debit cards are using the funds available on your checking account or savings account. Thus, in the very basic form of debit card, you can spend as much as you have on your accounts. Debit card offers you direct access to your checking account. Whereas, with the credit cards, you take a form of loan from the credit card issuer. In some cases, you could be approved an overdraft on your debit card.

How credit cards work?

After defining what are credit cards, and what is the difference between credit and debit card, what comes next is to see how credit cards work. There are some basic features of credit cards you should be familiar with. These are:

- Credit card is a form of loan.
- The credit card issuer will charge you an interest on the outstanding balance. Thus, you are paying interest on the money used.
- You have the obligation and you should pay the minimum repayment amount each month, failure to do so will result in paying penalty APR.

As it was mentioned earlier, the funds available on you credit cards can be considered as a form of loan. Thus, whenever you use your credit card, you are borrowing money from the credit card issuer. This means that you should pay back the outstanding balance, within the next month or during couple of months or years (depending on the terms and conditions). If you choose not to repay the full amount owed (balance) within a month (within the grace period to be more precise), you will be charged an interest rate. This interest is added on your account, and you are obliged to pay it.

When trying to understand how credit cards work, you should also know what credit limit is and how credit card is approved.

Credit limit – represents the maximum amount you have available on your credit card. Stated differently, it is the maximum amount of funds i.e. credit limit you can use (borrow) with your credit card. The maximum credit limit is determined by the bank on the basis of your credit card application.

In order for a credit card to be approved, the bank is evaluating your current employment position as well as past employment. In addition, you are evaluated on the basis of your income, your credit report and your credit history. From the aforementioned you should realize that your ability to service a credit card is analyzed. So, in general, the process for getting a credit card is as follows:

- Go through the numerous credit card offers.
- Decide on the most appropriate credit card for you.
- Read the credit cards terms and conditions.
- Read the terms and conditions once more (to make sure that you didn't miss anything).
- Fill out the credit card application.
- Credit card issuer will evaluate your ability to make payments on your credit card.
- The evaluation is based on your credit history, bill paying history, current outstanding debt, your monthly income, and your overall financial health.

- The credit card issuer makes a decision whether or not to approve a credit card.
  - If you are approved, you sign any additional documents, and voila, you are owner of a credit card.

You need to understand the process so as to avoid any uncomfortable situation, just because you didn't bother enough to understand how credit cards work. While, the aforesaid describes the process of getting a credit card, you should also know what to do with your credit card after approval.

Because you can use your credit cards in multiple ways, you should know what your obligations for using them are. Firstly, let's consider the different ways you could use your credit cards. You can use them for:

- Purchases – pay for your everyday purchases.
- Balance transfers – transferring your balance from an old credit card to a new credit card with lower APR.
- Cash advances – where you can withdraw money from an ATM.

After using your credit card in some of the ways listed above, you now have obligation each month. You should keep track of your items and purchases you have done during the month. This will ensure that you do not have any late payments, and get hit with a penalties. You can see all of your items for the past month in the monthly statement. Monthly statement – is recording your activity with your credit card. The monthly statement is sent by the credit card issuer. This report is sent on a monthly basis, and it shows all items i.e. activities for the previous month. Aside of the details about each amount spent, you can also see details about the interest charge added to your balance (as well as other charges). Moreover, you can see the minimum amount due, and the date it will be due. You can also see the billing cycle, and plan accordingly to benefit from the grace period.

Although credit cards are not complicated financial product, you do need to understand how credit cards work. This can ensure that you are using you credit card in the best possible manner. First, make sure you understand the specific credit card related terminology. Second, get familiar with the approval process. The most important thing, where many people have made a mistake, is the post approval period. The post approval period is the one where you actually use your credit card. Always have the adequate information before making any finance related decision.

2.4 Things to consider to better understand credit cards

Being able to use a credit card doesn't mean that you are good to go. As with everything else, you should primarily be focused on understanding credit cards. This is in a sense that you should understand how credit cards work, the characteristics of credit cards, different types of credit cards, etc. There are many things which should be comprehended before understanding credit cards. For this reason one starting point would be to be aware about the things you should know when it comes to credit cards.

You might ask – why understanding credit cards is important. Well, the answer is rather simple. You should have enough knowledge about credit cards, for the purpose of protecting yourself against any potential risk that come with the credit cards. One such a risk is to become over-indebted. Meaning that, if not used in the right manner, you can find yourself in a situation with high level of credit card debt. Moreover, keep in mind that credit cards are one of the most expensive form of debt. Thus, understanding credit cards will also help you to better cope with the credit card debt.

Having said that, some of the basic things you should know about credit cards are:

Debit card vs. credit card – is the first thing that should be understood. Namely, when using a debit card to pay for something, you are actually using the money available on your bank account. The limit on you debit card is the amount of money you have available on your own bank account.

With credit cards, on the other hand, you can spend up to the amount of credit limit approved by the issuer. Namely, when making purchase with a credit card, you are basically using issuer's money to pay for the goods. Afterwards, you have the obligation to pay back the used funds. Summing up, with debit card you are using your own money, while with credit card, you are using issuer's money.

Types of credit cards – there are couple of different types of credit cards available. They can be different in terms of the issuers, the intended purpose, the need for collateral, the place of usage, the available limit, etc. There are credit cards that can satisfy almost every potential need of credit card holder.

The number of credit cards you should have – is not clearly defined. Namely, the number of credit cards you should have will depend solely on your needs. Keep in mind that a general purpose credit cards will be adequate for almost all needs. But, again, the number of credit cards and type of credit cards you need will depend on your personal preference and situation. You can acquire a retail credit card for making purchases in your local every day store. Maybe a balance transfer credit card will help you to manage your high interest credit card debt.

Credit cards interest rates – an important thing that requires your attention. Namely, credit cards bear one of the highest interest rates. The interest rate and/or APR can be anywhere from 0% (introductory rate) up to nearly 30% (penalty APR). The interest rate you will be charged with depends on numerous factors such as: credit score, debt to income ratio, income level, payment history, credit inquiries, and type of credit card. These factors will be analyzed by the lenders before deciding on the APR you are going to be charged with. In addition, you should understand the different types of APR that can be charged, depending on the way in which you are using your credit card.

Signed contract is obligatory – thus always read your contract cautiously before signing. Once signed, the contract is binding for both sides, and it means that you consent to the terms and conditions defined by the issuer.

Credit line – is the amount of funds you have available on your credit card. The credit line is determined by the issuers. It can be standard for a specific type of credit card for all holders. Credit line can also be determined in accordance to the credit card applicant's qualifications.

The calculation method for interest rate – is another thing that should be considered. The interest rate can be calculated by averaging the daily account balance, and multiplying the figure with the periodic rate (periodic rate is calculated by dividing the APR with the number of days in a year).

Type of interest rate – can have major impact on your interest rate charge. There are two basic types of rates, fixed rate APR or variable APR rate. The fixed rate APR, as the name implies, is constant interest rate. Variable rate, on the other hand, is subject to changes because it is tied to an index (prime lending rate, LIBOR, etc.).

Grace period – represents the number of days you have available to pay off your balance in full, before interest is charged. The grace period can be from 20 to 30 days, depending on the issuer. If you pay the outstanding balance within the grace period, you will not be charged with interest. If you pay within the grace period, then it could be said that you have had interest free loan.

Credit card fees – can be substantial if you neglect them. Do not apply for a credit card with non-standard fees, and do not sign contract if fees are not clearly defined. The most common fees are: annual fee, balance transfer fee, foreign transaction fee, late payment fee, and a fee if you exceed your balance.

Revolving balance – no need to pay in full – because credit card is a form of a loan. You can choose either to pay your balance in full, or pay the minimum amount due for the billing cycle. Keep in mind though, that if you pay only the minimum amount due, you will be charged with interest rate on the balance you carry in the next month. The money you will pay on your credit card, can be reused again and again.

Minimum payments – represents the minimum amount you must pay each month. Paying the minimum amount will ensure that you do not damage your credit score and payment history. In addition, you will not be hit with a late payment penalty fee. The minimum payments can be calculated with the percentage method or the percentage + interest + fees method .

Credit cards and credit score – are in a close-fitting relation. Namely, credit cards can have positive or negative effect on your credit score in couple of different ways. When you have a credit card you can influence one of the most important credit score factor i.e. the payment history. Thus, failure to regularly pay your monthly payments could negatively impact your credit score, with penalty points for the payment history. Other factors that can have impact on your credit score are: credit utilization, average age of accounts, types of credit currently in use, etc.

Negotiate your fees – if you are a loyal customer, more importantly, if you are good customer. Contact your credit card issuer and ask for better terms if you have a high credit score. Tell the issuer that you can find better deals, and you are thinking to switch to another issuer with better terms.

Withdrawing cash at the ATM – can be done with a credit card. Namely, you can use your credit card at the ATM to withdraw cash, although you should avoid this. Try to avoid it because, withdrawing cash at the ATM with your credit card is rather expensive. The cash advance is charged with higher interest rates compared to the purchase interest rate.

Consumer rights – you are entitled to the consumer right as a card holder under the Truth in Lending Act. According to the Act, issuers are required to explain the contract terms. If you have problems with your bill, then you should be aware about The Fair Credit Billing Act. According to this Act, you are entitled the right to dispute and correct errors.

Credit cards are at the same time very useful and very dangerous financial product. They are a useful product because they could offer you numerous benefits. But, with credit cards you could very easily be in a situation of high levels of credit card debt. For the purpose of enjoying the benefits from credit cards, understanding credit cards is a must do. Always try to understand the different characteristics of this financial product. Collect information and knowledge before making a decision.

2.5 Basic types of credit cards offered by banks

Credit cards are one of the most used financial products offered by banks and other financial institutions. We use them in our everyday lives to pay for gasoline, buy groceries, or purchase some expensive items. They represent a form of a loan, a revolving credit to be precise. Which should be paid back, and the funds can be used again and again, until the card expires. After which the card should be renewed. Most probably you have at least one credit card with you at the time of reading this text. But do you know the different types of credit cards offered by the banks? Maybe you do maybe you don't. Whatever the answer, you should be familiar with the basic types of credit cards. You don't know whether you will need some of them in the future.

In addition, getting to know the different types of credit cards, you should also be able to understand how credit cards work. Credit cards can be highly useful product if used in the right manner. On the other hand, lack of understanding how credit cards work, could result in accumulation of credit card debt. An expensive debt that is.

Secured credit cards – as the name suggests, are credit cards issued on the basis of some collateral. Thus, secured credit cards are issued when a security deposit is put on the card. The deposit serves as a guarantee for the lender, in case you fail to repay your balance. In most cases, the amount of security deposit, determines the credit card limit. Although, you have put a deposit on your credit card, you should still make a monthly payment. Meaning that you should pay the minimum monthly payments stated in the agreement. This type of credit cards are usually used by people with no credit history. Secured credit cards are also used for the purpose of rebuilding credit history.

Unsecured credit cards – are widely used, because it does not require any form of collateral. The credit card limit is determined on the basis of applicants' credit history, and the ability to repay outstanding balance in accordance to the agreement.

Standard credit cards – also referred to as plain-vanilla credit cards, are a standard credit cards. These cards, don't provide you with any rewards. It can be said that because of this, they are also rather simple to understand.

Balance transfer credit card – is a card which provides you with a low introductory rate when making a balance transfer, from your old card to your new credit card. The introductory rate can vary from one credit card issuer to another. But it can go as low as 0% introductory APR rate. In addition, the low interest rate offer is valid for certain period of time. After the low interest period expires, the APR would be in accordance to the agreement terms.

Rewards credit cards – as the name indicates, are credit cards that provide an offer in the form of rewards on credit card purchases. They can be in the form of: cashback credit cards, reward in points and travel rewards. Which reward credit card you will choose, depends on your personal preferences and needs.

Student credit cards – are credit cards created in accordance to student's needs. Namely, this category of users, rarely have credit history, but they can benefit from having a credit card. In addition, student credit cards, can offer different forms of perks (rewards).

Charge credit cards – might not have any finance charge or minimum payment. This is so because, with charge credit cards you must repay the entire outstanding balance at the end of each month. Moreover, these cards do not have any limit. Failure to repay in full the outstanding balance will result in late payment fees. Furthermore, charge cards have a yearly fee, which could be higher than the other types of credit cards.

Subprime credit cards – are usually associated with applicants with bad credit history. Thus they bear rather high interest rate and fees, for which they are considered to be one of the worst types of credit cards.

Prepaid credit cards – are in some way similar to secured credit cards. Credit card owner should deposit money onto the credit card before using it. When a purchase is made using this type of credit cards, it is withdrawn from the card's balance. Unless you deposit more money onto the card, the limit is not renewed. This is the main difference with the secured credit cards. In addition, unlike secured credit cards, prepaid credit cards do not have finance charge or a monthly payment. Although referred to as a credit cards, do not use them to rebuild your credit. From its characteristics, it could be said that prepaid credit cards, are somewhat similar to debit cards.

Business credit cards – are credit cards issued to businesses. Namely, they are created to be used for business purposes. They come in handy for business owners, to separate between personal transactions and transactions made for the business.

Premium credit cards – can offer more benefits and rewards than the other types of credit cards. To be able to obtain a premium credit card (Platinum or Gold Cards) you should have an excellent credit history as well higher income level (the exact income level required depends on the card issuer). In addition, this type of credit cards offer higher credit limit and in some circumstances can bear a lower APR.

Co-branded credit cards – are credit cards issued on the basis of co-sponsorship by two companies. This form of credit cards offer benefits and rewards aimed specifically at the customers of the companies.

In today's economy, whatever need you have, most probably you will find a specific product to fulfill it. It is the same with your financial needs as well. This is especially true when talking about the different types of credit cards. The different types of credit cards are created to satisfy variety of financial needs for different customers. For instance, there is a credit card for people with no payment history, or credit card to separate your personal expenses with business expenses.

For this reason, it is important that you are familiar with the different types of credit cards available. You never know what financial need you will have to cover.

2.6 Understanding credit cards' APR – the cost of credit cards

Credit cards have become an integral part of our everyday life. We use credit cards for paying bills, making purchases, or simply as an emergency fund. This widespread usage of credit cards is imposing the need for gathering information and understanding different aspects related to the credit cards. One such aspect is for you to know what is and how does credit card APR works. Meaning that, you should understand the cost of funds available on your credit cards. Although it might look fairly simply, gaining in-depth understanding might cause some confusion..

Credit card APR defined

Annual percentage rate or APR in simple terms denotes the cost for using the funds available on your credit card. Meaning that, it is the yearly rate on your credit card paid for the outstanding balance. Although it is expressed on a yearly based, credit card companies are applying the APR to charge you on a monthly bases. There can be differences in the APR depending on the creditor or the characteristics of the borrower.

Types of Credit Card APR

For the purpose of understanding how does credit card APR work, you need to be familiar with the different types of credit card APR. Going through your credit card agreement you should notice that there might be different APR rates. The different rates are stated in the terms and conditions of a credit card. Therefore you need to know when different types of APR are applied. Their applicability depends on what you do with the available funds. Thus, you should distinguish between the following APR rates:

- Balance transfer APR – is the rate you pay in case you decide to transfer old credit card balance onto new credit card. Often you could find offers with low (even 0%) APR for a credit card balance transfer.

- Cash advance APR – credit cards can be used in many different ways and for different purposes. One such a purpose is cash advance i.e. withdrawal of funds from an ATM. If you decide to obtain funds through cash advance then you will be charged with this APR rate. You should be aware that this rate is usually one of the highest rates (compared to other APR rate, except the penalty rate). In addition, you do not have a grace period for the balance withdrawn at the ATM. As a consequence, cash advance can turn out to be very costly for you. try to avoid making cash advances.

• Purchase APR – this rate, as the name suggests, is applied when you make a purchase using your credit card.

• Penalty APR – failure to pay the minimum amount due for more than 60 days, will result in you being charged the penalty rate. Just to be clear, you will pay this rate on all the balances you have on your account. This rate is extremely unfavorable and it can be 29.9%, yes you could end up paying an APR of 29.9%.

Calculating monthly interest charge

Although you can find numerous calculators online to calculate your APR, try to understand the process of how your APR is calculated.

Let's say that your credit card has an APR of 16%, if you divide this by 365 (number of days in a year) then you will get the value for a daily APR to be 0.04385. If, for instance, your credit card balance is $2,000, the interest is added for the day, and the next day your balance is $2,000.87. The credit card issuer will multiply your current balance by the daily interest rate, for the purpose of finding out the daily interest charge. At the end of the next day the interest charge is added to your balance. This process is called compounding. In addition, the next day all other purchases are also added to the outstanding balance, while new payments are subtracted from the balance. The daily APR (and the compounding effect) is performed every day until the end of the monthly (billing) cycle.

If you want to know the reason why daily interest charge is preferred over a monthly interest charge, consider the length of each month. Because months have different length, credit card issuers, prefer to use the Daily Periodic Rate (DPR). This is the rate used in the example above, it can be calculated by dividing the APR by 365.
In order to obtain the interest for the month you should do the following calculation:

• Interest for monthly statement = Balance x DPR x days in billing cycle.

• Knowing that DPR is calculated by dividing the APR by 365, the formula can be written as:

• Interest for monthly statement = Balance x (APR/365) x days in billing cycle.

• The days in the billing cycle represent the number of days between two billing cycles.

After considering the APR and the daily periodic rate, what comes next is to see the role of credit card balance. Everyone is aware that the daily balance could change from day to day. This change could occur because of new purchases or money withdrawals, or when you make payments to your credit cards. For the reason that changes can occur in daily balance, banks and other financial institutions (credit card issuers) use various methods to calculate the balance. Mostly used methods to find the balance for which an interest should be charged are:

- Adjusted balance – when using this method the balance is calculated by subtracting the previous month's balance from the total balance. The difference is the remaining balance which represents the bases for interest charges.
- Average daily balance – when this method is used the daily balance is taken into consideration. When using this method, credit card issuers are adding up each month's daily balance and then divide the amount by the number of days in the month. This method is more popular with the credit card issuers when it comes to calculating the balance base for interest charge.

Grace period defined

Because of the importance of the grace period, and in order for you to understand how does credit card APR work, you must be familiar with the term. Before going to the credit card APR grace period, the term grace period should be defined. Namely, grace period is specific period after which the payment becomes due. Meaning that, if you make your payment within the grace period you will not be charged late penalties. When it comes to credit cards, banks are offering a grace period, a period during which they will not charge you any interest. This means, that if you pay off your outstanding balance during the grace period, you will pay 0% interest. This grace period is usually 25 days, so paying your balance within the period will save you money. Make sure you ask your credit card issuer about the billing cycle and the length of grace period. If you decide to pay the minimum amount due, then you will start paying interest on the outstanding balance (less the amount paid).

Therefore, many credit cards owners would like to know when the best time to make payments on their credit cards is. Well, before answering, it should be noted that paying at the right time could save you an interest charges. Meaning that the credit card issuer will not charge you any interest. The tricky part is that you need to have enough money to pay the full statement balance on time. So, when is the correct time to pay on time? In majority of cases, credit card issuers are giving you a grace period to pay the full statement balance. If you pay your balance in full during the grace period, you will not be charged an interest. Keep in mind that the grace period may not be applicable if you have cash advances. In this case, the credit card issuer might start calculating interest from the first day on balance withdrawn.

Factors affecting APR

When shopping around for a credit card, you must have noticed that the APR can be anywhere from 12% up to 23% (it can be higher or lower). Meaning that there could be a substantial difference in the APR you could be charged with. For this reason, you should understand the factors that determine the size of the APR you are going to pay. Some of the basic factors are:

• Your FICO score – or your creditworthiness, which has major impact on the APR you are going to pay. Because there are different APR's for different credit scores, your credit card terms and conditions might list several different APR's. These APR's are applicable to different credit score ranges. Thus, depending on whether you have excellent, average or bad credit score, you will be charged the applicable APR. Simply said the higher the FICO score the lower the APR. This means, that you should pay special attention to your credit score. Make periodical control of items in your credit score. Contact your credit bureau in case there are items recorded which should be removed.

• Another factor is the prime rate – which can be considered as a baseline interest rate. This baseline (reference) interest can change (fluctuate) in accordance to specific economic variables. Moreover, the prime rate is directly tied or related with the federal funds rate. The federal funds rate represent the rate paid by the banks for short term borrowing from the Federal Reserve. The prime rate is the federal funds rate plus 3 percentage points.

• Promotional offers – is yet another factor that could impact your credit card APR. Namely, periodically, banks have promotional offers on their credit cards. These promotional offers are one way for banks to attract new clients. Thus, make sure that you have gathered information about the promotional offers. One of the benefits from these offers is that you could be approved a credit card with lower APR for a certain period of time. In addition, you could enjoy a fee free credit card for a pre-determined period. Do not forget to collect information about the possible promotional offers.

Always keep in mind that when you pay interest, the purchased goods actually become more expensive. Try to understand how credit card APR works, because it can save you a lot of money in the long run. If, you pay back the outstanding balance on your credit cards within the grace period you will save interest charge. Also, try to understand the different types of APR. This can also save you money in the long run. Avoid, paying the penalty APR or cash advance APR, they are some of the highest you could be charged with.

2.7 Choosing the best credit card

Before going into more details regarding the way you should choose the best credit card, you should first get familiar with couple of other things. Namely, you should know the way credit cards work, the types of credit cards and the cost of credit cards debt.

When talking about credit cards we simply think of a card where we have certain credit to spend. The reality is not so simple though. Namely, there are numerous types of cards offered by banks. Credit cards can differ in terms of their purpose, benefits, issuing procedure, APR, fees, etc. Thus, the first thing before choosing your credit card should be to get familiar with the available types of credit cards.

Coming back to the process of selecting the best credit card. The process of choosing the best credit card for your needs and lifestyle imposes the need for couple of questions to be asked. The answer to these questions could be the starting point for the selection process of the best credit card. Therefore you should ask the following questions:

- Do you have credit card debt on multiple credit cards? Do you want to consolidate this debt? (Understand the balance transfer)
- Do you pay high interest rate on your current credit card(s) debt?
- Are you going to use the credit card to make purchases on a regular basis or you want to use it for cash purposes only?
- Do you travel on a regular basis? Is it by airplane or other means of transportation? Go through the different perks offered by credit card issuer.

By now, you should get some picture regarding the need you want to satisfy with your credit card. Meaning that you have decided on the purpose and the type of credit card you want. So, what's next?

Next step is to consider some other aspects related to your financial situation. For instance, see if you can really afford a credit card. Examine the way this form of potential debt will impact your monthly budget. On the basis of your credit score, check the interest rate you would pay on your new credit card. Low credit score is associated with higher cost (APR), meaning people with lower credit score have higher credit card cost.

After going through the issues above, the next logical step is to go through the process of choosing the best credit card.

Decide on the type of credit card needed

After answering the questions listed above you should ease the process of identifying the best credit card for you. Thus, before proceeding to other important aspects, you should decide on the type of credit card you will need. There are numerous types of credit cards offered by banks. Some of the basic credit cards types are:

- Balance transfer credit cards – can help you to reduce your interest cost especially if you take out 0% APR credit card or low interest rate balance transfer credit card.

• Credit cards which can help you rebuild your credit history – such as secured credit cards

• Rewards credit cards – offer different types of rewards some of which can be: cash back, rewards in points, and/or travel rewards

Deciding on the correct type of credit cards for your needs can provide several benefits in the future. Namely, if you use your credit card to make purchases on a regular basis, than cash back credit card might be beneficial. On the other hand if you decide to apply for travel credit card, then when you are making a purchase it won't do you much good.

Know your credit score

Knowing your credit score is important because you are able to find out the credit card promotions you are eligible for. Don't forget that higher credit score means better perks and credit card terms in general. Do you know why high credit score is preferred?. In case your credit score is lower than what you may have expected, try to go through the hassle and improve it.

Paying off the entire balance when due or not

The ability as well as the habit to pay off your outstanding balance in full each month is also an important factor to consider. Namely, think for a moment, do you usually pay off the entire credit card balance each month or not? Maybe you are using your credit card for pricey purchases and repay the balance through couple of billing cycles. In such a case the APR on your credit card is highly important. Namely, if you plan to gradually pay of the outstanding balance, then rewards credit cards might not be the adequate choice (usually these credit cards have higher APR).

Analyze your spending habits

It is important that you know your spending habits when it comes to credit card. If you see that you are making most of your purchases at the same place see if there is an offer for a co-branded credit card.

Apply for your credit card

This step is rather straight forward, you go to the bank of your choice and follow the application procedure. But, before applying, make sure that you have selected a credit card that offers the best value for you. For this reason, carefully consider the characteristics of the available credit cards. Remember, credit cards are one of the most expensive form of debt.

Although most of us don't like the credit card debt, having a credit card in your wallet can be beneficial. The benefits though, will come only if we make a clever selection of a credit card, and we manage the credit card debt wisely.

Before choosing the best credit card, always make sure that you know how you will use your credit card. In addition be familiar with the fees, interest rate, billing cycle, and other characteristics of the credit card you want to apply for.

Don't get into a situation where you end up with high level of expensive debt, simply because you have chosen wrong credit card.

2.8 How many credit cards are enough?

When the question about the number of credit card arises, the answer, one way or another, is associated with the FICO score. Most probably you are concerned about the influence of an additional credit card on your credit score. Although your credit score is highly important, being faced with the decision about the number of credit cards, there are other issues that should be taken into account.

Firstly, aside of the desire (or need for that matter) to increase your credit score, you need to know what will you do with the credit card(s) and do you really need a couple of credit cards or one or two will do for you. Having multiple credit cards is a time-consuming obligation, because you have to keep record for all of them, especially if you are using them in your everyday transactions. In addition, each credit card comes with a limit (line of credit), the more credit cards you have, the higher credit line you have available.

The aforementioned is intro into the second issue you should consider. Namely, you need to be aware about the psychological side of having increased consumption power (multiple credit lines). This is especially true for people having hard time to control their shopping "urges". Having high level of credit line can result in maxing out on the limit, since you do not spend any physical cash. In case you max out all of your credit card limit, most probably you will be faced with the vicious repayment circle. This is in a sense that you will be able to pay the minimum repayment on the outstanding amount on few credit cards, and then start withdrawing the same money to pay the minimum outstanding amount on the remaining credit cards. Keep in mind that an interest is paid along with the minimum amount. This means that, although you do pay the minimum amount, in reality you do not decrease the outstanding amount by the amount paid. In case you have not been captured by the vicious repayment circle (which is good) then you are faced with high interest expenses.

Coming to the reasons as to why do you want to hold more credit cards, putting aside the FICO related reasons. One reason would be to explore the benefits of "0" interest rate for the promotional period on purchases. If done correctly, utilization of this benefit is a smart thing to do, since you could buy on instalments, and repay the outstanding amount at the end of "0" APR period.

Credit cards could also be a helpful product in times of short-term decline in cash inflow, or unexpected cash outflows. In these situations you have two basic options, either to withdraw from your saving accounts or to find other means to raise the needed amount. For instance, borrow from relatives and friends (not recommended), apply for loan, or use your credit card(s). Taking out money from your saving accounts is not always a smart thing to do, because you might be faced with some penalties. Friend and relatives should be considered as lenders of last resort, the loan could be a valuable option, but the procedure for applying and obtaining the loan can take a few days (or even weeks). Therefore, having credit card could be considered a smart thing to do, especially in times of short-term need for cash or unexpected expenses.

It can be concluded that, aside of the FICO score related issues, the number of credit cards you should have depends on the reasons you have for having credit cards, as well as your personal behavior when knowing that you have line of credit that you can spend. In addition, do not forget the need to keep record for all of your credit cards, which can be time-consuming task, not difficult though.

2.9 Conclusion

By now it should be obvious that credit cards are at the same time one of the best financial products and one of the trickiest products which could cause financial distress. Which effect will dominate depends entirely on the credit card holder. While there are credit card holders enjoying the benefits, there also credit card owners who curse the day they have applied for a credit card.

In order for a credit card holder to be in the category of owners who enjoy the benefits, then better understanding of how credit cards work and the cost of credit card debt is a prerequisite. When dealing with the need to better understand credit cards, one should get familiar with the types of credit cards available, the need for credit cards as well as the importance of APR.

Before applying for a credit card, you should consider whether you really need a credit card or not. Next, you should define the criteria on the basis of which you will select the best credit card for you. This way you will make an informed decision regarding the selection and usage of your new credit card.

CHAPTER THREE:
LOAN PRODUCTS BASICS

3.1 Introduction

During our lives a need for having extra money might arise at some point. We could need larger amounts of funds to satisfy some major purchase (home, car, renovation, etc.) or maybe to cover some unforeseen expenses. This possibility will be imposing the necessity for acquiring these funds from somewhere. One option is to search through the products and services offered by the banking institutions.

Therefore we could apply for a bank loan in order to satisfy the need for additional money. Consequently, the need for getting familiar with the types of loans offered by banks is arising. It should be noted that there are numerous types of loans created for different situations. Loans offered by banks can differ from each other in terms of their maturity, need for collateral, usage, repayment, and purpose of the loan.

One major decision before applying for a loan is to select the most adequate loan. Getting the wrong loan can cost you money in the long run. Before applying for a loan, it would be valuable if you define what would be the most adequate loan in accordance to your income level, collateral level, life style, and the financial need you should satisfy.

3.2 Deciding about the most adequate loan

The process of gathering information regarding your search for a loan can be a time-consuming task. This is especially true if afterword's you realize that you have been gathering the wrong information. Not only it could be a time-consuming task, but it could also result in choosing inappropriate lender, which could have negative effect on your finances in the future. Thus, you could find out the hard way that in reality the best loan you have read about is not really the best loan for you.

Most probably, when you are shopping for a loan you will go online and start looking for the best mortgage, or the best car loan, or the best of whatever loan you need. This concept of gathering information and making decision, could, later on, turn out to be one of the worst mistakes you have made. Do you understand why? You can find information online about the best mortgage available. But did you ask the crucial questions, why is this the best mortgage and who is it best for, is it best for you?

It should be pointed out here that the most common mistake when shopping for a loan is that we all shop for the best loan. Instead, of gather information and look for the best loan for us personally, the most appropriate loan in accordance to our needs and desires.

Consequently, before you start gathering information about the best loan, make sure that you have understand the main aspects associate with almost every loan. The crucial point is that you understand the basics of the loans, instead of understanding the offers about the best loan. Do not try to understand the best loan placed in front of you on your screen. Instead, try to understand the things you should be informed about, before chosing the best lender and/or loan. You might wonder, when looking for the best loan, what are the basic issues that you should be familiar with. First and foremost, the most important issue is for you to understand that you are looking for the best loan for you. Do not fall in the trap of accepting the loan which has been heavily promoted, it doesn't necessary means that this is the best loan for you. Coming back to the aspects you should be informed about in relation to the loans, they are:

- Inform your-self about the *interest rate* related issues – there are two things that should be considered when talking about the interest rates. Namely, you should be aware that the interest rate could be fixed or variable. Thus, you need to gather information about the advantages and disadvantages that come with a fixed interest rate loan and variable interest rate loan. Consequently, you should decide whether you want your loan to bear a fixed or variable interest rate. In addition, you should also know that a loan has an *interest rate and annual percentage rate* or APR. You can find ads promoting the lowest interest or low APR, but do you really know what the difference is.

• Always know you *credit score* before you start shopping for a loan. This is important issue because, high credit score could enable you to get a loan with lower interest rate. It could give you a certain degree of negotiation power with your creditor. Every lender is looking for a credit-worthy borrower. Try to use your advantage for your own benefit.

• Another thing to consider is the *debt-to-income ratio,* since it is an important indicator about your financial health. Make sure that you understand the debt to income ratio and calculate yours as well before shopping for a loan. Hence, you would know the maximum amount of debt you could afford.

• The repayment period or *loan term* is yet another subject that should be taken into consideration. You should be aware about the effect arising from a different loan term on your financial health as well as living standard. Namely, repaying your loan in a shorter time could potentially result in savings on interest rate charges, but could mean higher monthly payments. Subsequently, the *monthly payment* is another point to be considered. Most often you can find info about how much mortgage can you afford, or how much loan can you afford. But the thing that should additionally be of interest for you is how much you want your monthly payment to be. Although your credit score along with the debt to income could show that you can afford higher monthly payment, it doesn't mean that you should take the maximum loan, especially if you do not need so much funds.

• Knowing all additional *charges and fees* is of crucial importance for you. Don't put yourself in a situation where you pay hidden fees just because you didn't asked your lender everything. These fees can be substantial if you have a loan with longer repayment period.

• The *collateral requirement* – among other things, you should also know whether or not the lender is asking for some type of collateral. Namely, you should know that a lender can offer secured or unsecured loan. The first being a loan where you should provide some form of assets as a guarantee that you will pay back the loan.

• Maybe the most important thing for easier comparison is the *cost of credit.* The cost of credit is providing an information about the full cost of the loan you are going to take. One way to find the cost of credit is to multiply the amount of your monthly payments by the number of payments you will have and add all fees and charges you will have to pay. Then subtract the principal amount of the loan. The number you will get is the cost of your credit. Simply stated, the cost of borrowing is the difference between the principal amount you borrow and the total amount you will have to repay your borrower by the end of the loan term. It could be said that the cost of credit is a good measure to see the real cost of the money you are planning to borrow.

When it comes to taking a loan, you should always consider the financial and non-financial issues. Though there are things that could have impact in terms of the cost of your loan (interest rate, credit score, etc.), there are also issues that will have effect on your living standard as well as life style. Never take out a loan in a situation in which you are not informed adequately, never rush to get a loan. Don't be eager, make sure you have answered all the necessary questions before applying for loan. Do not fall in the best loan trap, look for the best loan for you.

3.3 Basic types of loans available

Like it or not, most of us have or will take a loan sometime in the future. Although, maybe you don't want to have a loan, the fact is that during a specific period of your life, or a period of financial distress, you will need a loan. That is unless you belong to rich and wealthy category of people. Therefore, n order for you to be better safe than sorry, you should primarily inform yourself about the different types of loans that could be found out there. Try understanding the basic features of the different types of loans. Meaning, that you should grasp the logic of the characteristics behind the general loan categorization and specific loans.

Again, before applying for a loan, you should sit down and consider the different possibilities you have at your disposal. Namely, you should make sure that you know the different types of loans. Understanding the loans will help you make a better and informed decision regarding a loan that will be suitable for your needs, which is second key issue to remember. Meaning that, you should know the reasons because of which you are taking a loan. Thus, it would be much easier for you to select the best loan when shopping around.

The need for gathering information is to ensure that you will have the best loan with the best terms in accordance to your life style and financial situation. Always remember that some loans are more expensive than others.

Prior to the explanation of the types of loans, you should be able to define what is loan. A loan is the process in which one entity is giving money or other form of asset to another entity. The money or assets, are given with the expectations for future repayment of the principal amount, plus an interest or other form of charges. Thus, do not expect that you will get free money, you must pay back your loan plus the interest you are charged with.

If you are not aware that there are numerous types of loans, then you might get confused. Consequently, it could be said that loans can be categorized in accordance to couple of factors, basically representing crucial characteristics of the loan. Thus, the different types of loans could be categorized in terms of the following factors:

- The need for collateral
  - Unsecured loans
  - Secured loans
- Repayment terms and terms for reusing of funds
  - Open-end credit
  - Close-end credit
- Time to maturity
  - Short-term debt
  - Intermediate-term debt
  - Long-term debt
- Loan purpose
  - Loan approved for a specific purpose
    - Buying a home (mortgage loan)
    - Buying a car – car loan
    - Buying in store – Consumer loan
  - Loans for general use (no specific purpose)
    - Personal loan
    - Credit card
  - Loans according to their interest rate
    - Variable rate loans
    - Fixed rate loans

On the basis of the whether a loan needs a collateral or not, we can distinguish two basic types of loans, secured and unsecured loans.

Secured loans (collateral loans) – a loans that are tied up against some form of asset. This way the lender is ensuring that the loan would be paid back, in case you fail to meet your monthly obligations. The underlying asset is referred to as a collateral or guarantee. This implies that, in case of a loan default, the lender has the right to repossess the asset and cover the loan. Due to the fact that the lender is protected against non-repayment of loan, interest rates on secured loans tend to be lower compared to interest rates on unsecured loans.

Unsecured loans – unlike secured loans, with unsecured loans you do not need to provide asset as a collateral. These loans are approved on the basis of your credit score and credit history, as well as the level of your income. Because these loans, are not guaranteed with an assets, they usually have higher interest rates. They are perceived by the lenders as riskier types of loans.

Taking into consideration the loan repayment terms, a difference among various types of loans can be found. This is taking into consideration the possibility to reuse the repaid amount. Meaning that, some types of loans have a revolving characteristics, while, other loans, do not offer this possibility. In line with the aforementioned, the loans can be placed in two categories, open-end credit and close-end credit.

- Open-end credit – this type of consumer credit is also referred to as a revolving credit, because of the way it can be used. The revolving credit, can be used continuously for purchases. The outstanding amount is repaid back on a monthly basis, either in full or portion of the outstanding debt. An example for a well know product that falls in the category of open-end credit are the credit cards. In addition, home equity lines of credit (HELOC) belong to this category. These loans have a so-called credit limit, representing the maximum amount you could borrow at once. You are not obliged to use the entire limit at once, you can use the available funds, as you need.

- Closed-end credit – is most often used as a means of financing a specific intent during a specific period of time. The closed-end credit is also referred to as an installment loans because of its repayment obligation. Namely, consumers have a pre-defined payment schedule and are obliged to make a regular payment. The most common payment schedule is the monthly schedule. Consumers are charged an interest rate until the full repayment of the principal amount. The interest rate charged can be different among lenders as well as borrowers, because of the importance of borrowers' credit score. Some examples of a closed-end credit are: mortgage, car loans, appliance loans, etc.

Loans can be classified from the "time" point of view. In other words, not all loans have the same maturity date. Meaning that, they differ in terms of their repayment period. Hence, in accordance to the repayment period, there are three basic categories: short-term loan, intermediate-term loan, and long-term loan. The short-term loan is a loan that should be repaid in one year or less. The intermediate-term loan is commonly characterized with a repayment period of anywhere from one year to five years. The long-term loans are considered to be loans with maturity period of more than five years, but most often they have a repayment period of ten years and more.

Another categorization of the loans can be performed with reference to the purpose of the loan. Namely, if you want to renovate your house, or purchase some appliance, you could find a loan designed specifically for these purposes. On the other hand, you could apply for a loan without having any specific purpose in mind (yes this is hardly the case, since you always know why you take the loan). For instance, you could take a loan (no specific purpose loan) to pay for some unexpected expenses.

Furthermore, loans can be classified on the basis of the type of interest rate they have. Namely, a loan could be assigned with a variable interest rate or a fixed interest rate.

- A variable interest rate loan is considered to be a loan where the interest rate applicable to the outstanding balance can change in accordance to the variations in market interest rates. Meaning, that the interest rate is adjusting to the market interest rate. Thus you could end up paying much higher or much lower interest rate on your loan, regardless of the interest rate at the time of signing the agreement.

- On contrary, fixed interest rate loan, is characterized as a loan in which the interest rate remains the same through the life of the loan. Meaning that, regardless of the movements in the market interest rates, you are paying fixed interest rate on your loan. With other words, you will pay the interest rate that has been agreed upon at the time of signing the loan agreement.

The aforementioned types of loans are based on the classification taking into consideration the general loans features. Aside of this classification, there is one more classification i.e. the types of loans as they are offered by the banks and other financial institutions. For that reason, there is a need for some of these loans to be listed and briefly explained. Accordingly, the different types of loans are briefly explained in the subsequent lines.

- Student loans – are loans available to college students and their families. The purpose of student loans is to serve as help for the payment of higher education costs i.e. tuition fees. The basic form of student loans are: federal student loans and private student loans. Most often federal student loans are preferred, because of the lower interest and better repayment terms.

- Mortgages – are a form of loans used for buying a homes. Because of consumers' inability to pay the price of the home in full at the time of buying the home, they are in need of additional funds. These funds are obtained through a mortgage loan. You should know that mortgage loan is associated with your home, thus failure to meet your monthly payments could result in foreclosure of your assets (collateral). In addition, mortgages loans are considered to be loans with lowest interest rates. There are different types of mortgage loans you should be aware about.

- Auto loans – have similar characteristics with mortgage loans, in terms of the need for collateral. In other words, auto loans are tied to your property (most often the vehicle you will purchase). Failure to meet your payments, could result in losing your vehicle.

- Personal loans – are loans used for various (as the name suggests) personal expenses and/or needs. This type of loan is not approved for some specific reason, as it was the case with mortgage or auto loans. Personal loans can be used for repaying your outstanding debt (most often credit card debt), aiming at reduction of the interest rates though balance transfers. The terms for approval of these loans are tightly related to borrowers' credit score. Personal loans represent an unsecured loan. Make sure that you know the things you should consider before applying for a personal loan.
- Payday loans – are short-term loans, characterized with high interest rates. These loans are usually used to overcome short-term cash flow problems. Payday loans come with certain benefits and drawbacks.
- Consolidation loans – are loans commonly used to better manage your finances. You are taking this type of loan to consolidate all (or most) of your debts into one single loan, and one single monthly payment. You could also get a better deal in terms of lower interest rate.
- Home equity loans – if you have some portion of equity in your home, it means that your home is worth more than you owe on it. This difference, called equity, can be used for paying more costly projects. For this reason, they are used for renovating your home, consolidating debt, etc.
- Home equity lines of credit (HELOC) – are somewhat similar to the home equity loans, since they both use the equity in your home as a mean of loan guarantee, thus having lower interest rates. The difference between the aforementioned type of loan and HELOC is in the repayment terms as well as the type of interest rate. That is, home equity loan is characterized with fixed interest rate and regular payments. On the other hand, HELOC is consisted of a variable interest rate and flexible payment schedule.

After you got acquainted with the different types of loans, you should be able to identify the most appropriate loan which will serve your needs in the best manner. Understanding different features of different types of loans would make the shopping for loans much easier. In addition, you should always know your rights as a consumer. You can apply for loan for the purpose of buying a car, purchasing a home, paying your tuition fees, renovating your home, etc. There is a wide range of loans available to cover different needs. Thus, for the purpose of ensuring safe lending practices and eliminating the possibility for manipulation of borrowers, a federal guidelines have been set in place. In that manner, you should know that irrespective of the type of loan and its repayment terms, every loan is overseen by state and federal guidelines for the protection of consumers. If you think that you have been manipulated or misinformed, then feel free to check your rights at the Federal Trade Commission.

3.4 Getting familiar with the different types of credit

Credit represents an agreement between the borrower and the lender. The borrower is given certain value, with the obligation to repay the same later on. Most forms of credit bear interest, and you are charged accordingly. There are different types of credit offered by banks and other lenders. The credit can differ in terms of its purpose (personal loan, credit card, mortgage), the way it functions (revolving or non-revolving), payment structure, and the need for collateral.

Credit cards

Credit card is one of the most used forms of credit. This form of credit is offering the convenience for users to borrow money from their bank or a credit card issuer. Credit cards can be used for purchases and for withdrawals of cash, and there are different types of credit cards available depending on the purpose or the issuer. This form of credit is also called revolving credit because of the way in which the available credit is repaid and reused.

Bank loans

Loans are another form of credit available for customers. This form of credit can be in the form of loans repaid through monthly installments for a pre-defined time frame. This credit type is not a revolving, because, the repayment of principal is final, and cannot be reused as it is the case with credit cards. In order for new credit limit to be available, you should go through the application process and get approved again. There are different types of loans, depending on the purpose they are used for (mortgage, car loan, etc.), the need for collateral, the target customer group, etc.

Overdrafts

Overdrafts are form of credit which allows you to withdraw money even when your account balance is zero. The overdraft limit is defined by the bank on the basis of your account history, income, spending habits and needs.

Higher purchase loans

Higher purchase loan is a form of credit which is aimed at the possibility for purchasing goods. In accordance to the agreement of this type of credit, purchased good will be owned by the borrower, once the purchase amount is paid back. In case, you have late payments, creditors can ask for the goods back.

Secured credit

This credit is a form of credit backed by some form of collateral. The type of collateral needed, to some extent, depends on the type of loan. For instance, a mortgage loan commonly is guaranteed by the property purchased, or some other property. Car loan can be backed with the car purchased. In case the borrowers is not servicing its credit regularly, creditors, can take possession of the collateral.

Unsecured credit

Unsecured credit is opposite of secured credit. Meaning that, with the unsecure credit you don't need a collateral. Stated differently, unsecured credit is not guaranteed by a collateral. In case of borrowers default, the credit will not be paid back.

Non-revolving credit

This form of line of credit is usually referred as an installment credit. With this type of credit you should pay a fixed monthly payment. The payment is made until the principal amount is paid in full. Example of a non-revolving or installment credit is mortgage. You cannot reuse the funds over and over again. Once you make the payment, the principal amount is reduced.

Revolving credit

As it has been mention, credit cards a one of the best representatives of revolving credit. Having a revolving credit means that you have a certain amount of credit limit available. You can access these funds whenever you want, and use them over and over again. You are obliged to pay the minimum amount on your outstanding balance defined each month.

Service credit

A type of credit where the outstanding balance should be fully repaid at the end of the month. With this type of credit your debt is not transferred to the next month. In addition, the outstanding balance is not repaid through installments. Some examples of service credit are: cell phone accounts, utilities or charge cards. In most cases this form of credit is not recorded on your credit report.

Short-term credit

A payday loan can be a good example of a short-term credit. This form of credit is secured against your next paycheck. The downside of short-term credit is that it is relatively expensive form of credit. Interest rates on short-term credit can be up to couple of hundred percent.

Understanding the different types of credit available will ensure that you will choose the most adequate one for your needs. In addition, having different types of credit accounts on your credit report is demanded by the lenders. It shows that you are able to cope with different accounts and manage your finances accordingly. The different types of credit you have are capturing 10% of your credit score. Consequently, you should try to have a various credit accounts in your payment history.

3.5 Conclusion

Because of the possibility that we might need a loan at some point in our life, it would be a wise move to try to understand the basics. Whether you have a loan or you plan to apply for one, it is important that you get acquainted with the basics behind the functioning and the benefits and drawbacks of loans.

Knowing the different types of loans will ensure that you have applied for the most appropriate loan to satisfy your specific need. Of course, we should start by identifying the reasons why we want to take out a loan. Do we need extra funds to purchase a car, to buy a home, or we want to renovate our home? There is a type of loan which will cover almost every need we could think of.

For this reason, it is of utmost importance to decide on the best loan in accordance to our needs and life style and the type of loan. This way we will be managing the loan, not the other way around. We don't want to be in a situation in which our lives are dictated by inadequate debt levels. Which could happen if we have inadequate loans.

CHAPTER FOUR:
COPING WITH YOUR DEBT

4.1 Introduction

Talking about bank products and services it is inevitable that the topic about debt will arise. Although nobody wants to have debt, there is high probability that we might have debt at some point in our life. Irrespectively of the reasons we have acquired debt, the fact is that we should find adequate strategy to manage it.

Coping with our debt is one of the most important aspects in our finances. On one hand failure to properly manage our debt or neglecting it can result in worsen financial health. On the other hand, if we cope with our debt wisely, it can offer numerous benefits. Thus, the necessity to deal with our debt is imposing the requirement for getting familiar with some of the basic strategies for getting out of debt.

These strategies can help in the debt repayment process. They can help in situation in which someone is overindebted or simply when someone wants to pay off its debt faster. There are different strategies depending on your type of debt. But when talking about bank products and services your debt can be in one of the two general categories: credit card debt or loans. One commonly used method for managing your debt is to refinance your existing loans. Accordingly, the basics related behind loan refinancing will be part of this chapter. Though debt refinancing could be used for both categories, credit card debt can be managed with another strategy as well. Namely, credit card balance transfer can be used to pay off your credit card debt with minimum or no interest rate charge. That is, as long as the credit card debt is repaid in full in accordance to the agreed terms.

4.2 Basic strategies for paying off loans faster

Before reading the strategies there is one thing that should be clarified. Namely, the financial state you are currently in. There are two possible situation you could be in if you are planning to get out of debt. The first situation is that you are over-indebted. Over indebted means that you are not able to meet your monthly financial obligations, even though you have lowered your standard of living. The second situation is that you are in good financial condition. You have an increase in your monthly income or you have accumulated capital and you can be debt free. Stated differently you are in a good financial standing and you are making enough money to maintain a stable lifestyle and have an extra income that could go for loan repayment. The situation you are in could significantly impact the strategy to get out of debt. These strategies are for you if you are in the second situation. If you are in the first category, the strategies are a bit different.

Before continuing, when deciding to pay off loans, do not consider cashing your saving account or 401 (K) plan. This strategy should be the last repayment resort. Meaning that, cashing in on your saving accounts or 401(K) plan could be done only, and only, if you are over indebted. Only when you are no longer able to pay all of your financial obligations on time. Otherwise, you should not use this capital to pay off loans. Be aware that at some point you will retire. Using your savings and accumulated capital to pay off debt early in life, could leave you without any retirement income.

The reason for your desire to get yourself out of debt is also an important factor. This factor is influencing your future decision regarding the repayment strategy. You might want to get out of debt faster because you have enough accumulated capital or an increase in your monthly income. Consequently, aying off a loan will not affect your life style or living standard. Meaning that, you could maintain your spending level even though you are repaying your debt early. Another reason you might want to get out of debt is that it negatively influences your lifestyle. This is in a sense that your monthly financial obligations are taking up big portion of your monthly income. Do not confuse this situation with an over indebted one. Unlike over indebted person, you have no problem to meet your monthly obligations. The problem is that you are forced to adapt your lifestyle, and limit your spending. In this case maybe your strategy should include a consolidation loan.

Although there are many, get out of debt, strategies, it could be said that maybe the best strategy is the strategy that will be combination from different strategies. The combined strategy is defined using the best characteristics of two or more strategies. Combining different strategies enables you to have a strategy that will be appropriate for your situation both financially and psychologically. Thus the best strategy is the one that is most suitable for your income level, spending habits, spending and saving behavior, etc.

One of the simplest strategy is to divide your monthly installment into a **biweekly payment**. Making a biweekly payments, will decrease the cost of your loan. You will be able to save on the amount of interest paid. The saving in interest expense is possible because you are speeding up the repayment of the principal amount. Look at the illustrative example in the following two tables. The calculations are made for a loan of $150,000.00 with term of 15 years and 4.5% interest rate.

Loan amount	Monthly	Pay off	Interest
$150,000.00	$1,147.49	15 year -1	0.0

In this example the monthly payment is $1,147.49 and the loan is repaid in 15 years and 1 month, and you do not have any interest saved. You pay the full interest. On the other hand, look at the second table. The calculations are made for the same loan, with one difference, instead of monthly payment, the calculation is made on the basis of bi-weekly payment.

Loan amount	Be-weekly	Pay off date	Interest
$150,000.00	$573.75	13 year – 6	$ 6,031.89

From the second table you can notice two very important facts. The first one is the payoff date, making a bi-weekly payment will reduce the repayment period by 19 months. Second, did you notice the interest saving? Making a be-weekly payments has saved you $6,031.89 in interest expense. At the same time, you did not increase your overall monthly payment, you simply split it in two separate payments. Consult your loan officer about the effect from a bi-weekly payments on the repayment period and interest savings on your debt. Perform the informative calculations on your loan and decide accordingly.

Rounding up your monthly payments is yet another relatively simple strategy. This strategy is helping you to get out of debt faster. The strategy is straight forward to apply. If your monthly installment is for example $255, you could round it up to $300. The $45 difference will go toward the repayment of the principal amount. At the end you will repay your loan faster i.e. before the maturity date.

Pay every month **more than the minimum**. This strategy is also a quite simple and easy to understand strategy. Till certain extent this strategy is similar to the rounding up strategy. When applying this strategy, you should basically increase your monthly payment. For instance, if your monthly obligation is $300, you could increase it and pay for example $400 or $500. The amount you will pay above the minimum installment is up to you to decide. Make the decision of how much extra you will pay based on your monthly income and spending habits. This strategy will reduce the time it will take you to repay your loan because you are repaying the principal amount faster. The more you pay above the minimum, the faster you are repaying your loan.

The aforementioned simple strategies could (should) be used if you have one or two loans. In case you have multiple debts with different size then you should consider combining the characteristics from some of the strategies explained in the next lines. Before defining and selecting your get out of debt strategy you should do one crucial thing. That is to analyze you spending habits. If you spend money on things you do not need, stop immediately.

Now, going back to the strategies, you need to take two steps. The first step is to rank your debts according to their interest rate – highest to lowest. The second step is to rank your loans according to their amount – lowest to highest. This way you are becoming aware about the interest rate (and interest amount) you are paying on each debt. Also, you are becoming aware about the size of each loan. After you have ranked your loans according to the previous steps you could examine the strategies.

One strategy you could apply to get out of debt is to focus on **paying off loans with the highest interest rate first**. After paying of the most expensive debt, transfer the available funds to paying out the second most expensive debt, and so on. This way you will gradually eliminate the debt that is eating up large amount of money towards interest payment. Keep in mind that you should transfer the funds from the repaid loan towards the repayment of the second most expensive loan, and so on.

Another method is to use the ranking of your debts from **lowest debt to highest debt in terms of their size**. According to this strategy you should start by paying off the smallest debt first. As you repay one loan, you are transferring the available funds toward the repayment of the second loan on the list, and so on. This strategy can be a bit tricky if you have debts with different interest rate. Since you might end up paying high level of interest if you have large debt with high interest rate. This is so because the sizable debts would be ranked last on the list. Consequently, they would be last in the repayment systems. If the debt is bearing a higher interest rate then you will pay this interest for longer period before full repayment of the debt. This method might be suitable if the interest rate you pay on all of your debts is more or less similar.

Apply for **debt consolidation loan** is also another strategy. It could be said that this strategy may not get you out of debt faster. Instead, this strategy could help you to decrease the number as well as the size of your monthly installments. Stated differently, you will take a new loan to repay all of your existing loans. Combining multiple installments into one monthly (or biweekly) installment. Meaning that you will consolidate all of your loans (debts) into one bigger loan, and improve your money management. This is so because you will have only one monthly payment (installment) which is much easier to keep record of than having multiple monthly payments on multiple loans. In addition, the consolidation loan can serve as a protection against taking on an additional loans. Moreover, getting a consolidation loan, can reduce your monthly payment, thus enabling you to even save a portion of your income, and help you accumulate an emergency fund.

One strategy is to speak with a **financial advisor**, especially if you do not have any financial background or you have difficulties in understanding the financial processes. This is not so much of a strategy as it could be smart thinking. It is smart because you will define repayment strategy with someone who understands the financial process in-depth. The strategy will be tailored in accordance to your financial situation. Also, financial advisor could ensure that you stick to your strategy. The drawback from using a financial advisor is that it can be a relatively expensive. People are not willing to pay high price for counseling. Keep in mind that financial advisors could be beneficial because they are aware about the possible products that you could use, and have the needed information.

Regardless of the strategy you decide to use to repay your debt(s) in full, you should keep paying the minimum amount on all debts in accordance to the agreed terms. When defining your strategy, make sure that you have taken into consideration all relevant factors, and set a loan repayment goal. This would ensure that you have an adequate strategy and a goal to measure the effectiveness of your strategy.

4.3 The decision whether or not to pay off a loan early

It is difficult to find a person who doesn't have any form of debt, whether it is a car loan, credit card, personal loan or mortgage the probability is that almost every one of us have it. It could be said, though, that nobody likes having a loan, but the cruel reality is that at some point in our lives we will have to have it. Unless we are prepared to pause our purchases until we save enough to buy a car, a house, or other items we would like (until we are old enough to retire, because then we will have enough money accumulated). So we do have a loan, the next step is to go through the process of paying off a loan before its maturity. Should you pay off your loans?

Although nobody likes having debt, we should also considered the reason why we have debt. If the reason is that we have taken a loan to purchase (invest) in a necessary goods such as: car, renovation, or purchase a house, than it is good to have a loan. Maxing out your credit card limit to purchase unnecessary things, or to party all night long, is one of the worst ways to manage your finances. Why? Because, aside of the short-term satisfaction that you have when buying a piece of jewelry, or cloths, what remains in the long run is your debt. Short term pleasure has been transformed into long-term obligation ascertain with decreased liquidity and increased costs.

Things to consider before paying off a loan

Regardless of the reason you have had for taken a loan, the fact remains that you have a loan, and you should repay that loan. The question then becomes – Should you be paying off a loan earlier? There is no simple answer to this question. The complexity in answering the question is imposing the need to carefully analyze couple of issues:

- The existence of penalty for early repayment;
- The interest rate charge – or saving for that matter;
- The time period of additional funds available;
- Alternative use of available funds – should you invest them;
- The effect of early repayment on your credit score;
- Repayment strategy;

Before proceeding in-depth about the aforementioned issues, one thing should be considered. Before even thinking about paying off a loan, you should have an emergency fund. This fund should help you to bridge over any unforeseen expenses, or even survive the unemployment period, in case you find yourself unemployed. There is no clearly define rule regarding the size of the fund, but very often it is said that it should be enough to cover six month expenses. In some cases it is said that the fund should be equal to six months of income. The later making more sense, because that way you could retain your life style (at least for six month without any income). Off course, the size of the emergency fund at the end is your decision.

Coming back to the issues that should be considered before paying of a loan. You should consider the **expenses** as well as any additional income you could generate (saving the interest payment) when repaying your loan. Meaning that primarily you should see if there are any penalties or charges for early repayment. Some institutions charge an early repayment fee. The amount of the fee varies from institution to institution but you should definitely take it into account. Secondly, you should estimate the money you will **save if you pay off your loan earlier**. This is in terms of interest rate you would otherwise pay if decide not go for early repayment. This is closely related with the alternative use of available funds. Meaning that you should analyze if you could invest those money in interest earning instrument or an instrument that will provide you with a return. In addition, you should analyze the money you could be earning if you decide to invest your money in a CD, the stock market or any other high yield instrument.

Before paying of a loan, you should take into account the **durability of the available funds** you have on hand. In other words, do you have additional funds for a short period of time, or the increased availability of funds will proceed in the future. This is important because if you make a commitment for early repayment or faster repayment of your loan, you should be sure that you will have available funds in the future. In case you have extra money this month because of some bonus or some extra activity you got paid for, then by no means should you consider early repayment.

Considering the effect, from paying off a loan, on your **credit score**. Noteworthy is to mention that it will have positive impact. Meaning that if you pay off your debt before maturity it will show a stability in your behavior for managing your finances i.e. financial obligations.

Another thing to consider before paying off a loan is the **repayment strategy**. There are a couple of basic strategies that you could apply, such as increasing the monthly payment strategy, or a lump sum payment strategy, etc.

The benefits arising from paying of your debt faster are:

• Saving the amount of interest expense you would have during the remaining life of your debt;

• Improving your credit score for any future needs for loan;

• Increase the availability of funds in the future because you do not have any monthly installment;

• Free up funds so you could accumulate capital for future purchases, in case you can save the amount you would otherwise pay as installment.

The drawbacks arising from paying of your debt faster are:

• Possibility to end up paying an early repayment penalties;

• Tying up available capital;

• Wrong analysis about your future income and capital needs could result in applying for new loan in short period of time, thus end up paying the interest rate "twice'. This is in a sense that in many cases at the beginning of the repayment period big portion of the monthly payments is assigned to the interest payment and certain portion goes toward principal payment. Thus, paying loan before maturity date means that you have paid big portion of the interest. In case you need to take on a new loan, you will again start from beginning and thus have to pay higher amount of interest.

• You don't get to use the extra money you have in hand.

It could be stated that the decision for paying of a loan early should not be taken for granted. This decision could have strong (positive or negative impact) on your financial future. Thus, before making the decision to pay off debt earlier always take into consideration all relevant aspects and issues. Also, always consider the advantages and disadvantages that will come with the repayment of a loan before its maturity. Along with your ability to pay off your debt earlier and the effect on your life style should always be taken into account as well.

4.4 Loan refinancing basics – things to consider

The last couple of years are marked with an increased interest in loan, especially mortgage refinancing. This activity is primarily due to the decrease in loan interest rates. Having the opportunity to lower the mortgage interest rate, homeowners rushed into refinancing their original mortgage. This is so because original mortgage would have been with (much) higher interest rate. After refinancing, homeowners were able to make substantial savings. But what is loan refinancing?

In simple words refinancing a mortgage is the process of applying for a new mortgage which will replace the existing mortgage. The same applies for any type of loan being refinanced. It could be defined as the process or a method through which you obtain new mortgage with the objective of lowering your interest rate, reducing monthly payment, cash in on your equity or change mortgage terms. These are the most common reasons, there are other reason as well.

You can chose to take new mortgage from the same bank (or lender) or from another bank. The important thing to remember here is that you can try to negotiate with your current lender (especially if you have good credit score). But, also, don't forget to shop around for better terms.

There are different reasons as to why people would like to refinance their mortgage. One reason might be the need for lowering the monthly payments. Lowering the cost of the mortgage loan is yet another reason why people refinance their mortgage. Some of the most common reasons to refinance a loan are:

• Better interest rates – is one of the main reason as to why people refinance their mortgage. Namely, they are able to make substantial savings by refinancing original mortgage at lower interest rate. The lower interest rate can be due to improved credit score, or simply decrease in market interest rates because of economic activity.

• Convert variable interest rate into lower fixed interest rate – another reason to refinance your mortgage is the desire to convert from adjustable to fixed interest rate. If you refinance your mortgage in time of low interest rates, you can lock in the interest rate. In addition you can eliminate the insecurity in the level of monthly payments, which comes with the variable interest rate.

• Lower monthly payment – for some reason you might want to lower your monthly payment. One way to do it would be through refinancing.

• Reduce mortgage term – there are people which can afford to pay higher monthly payment couple of years after they have taken the mortgage. For this reason, they are refinancing their mortgage at a higher monthly payment (not necessarily) to reduce the repayment period of their mortgage. This way they will pay off their mortgage much faster and in a shorter period of time.

• Cash out on your equity – is a reason to refinance your mortgage if you want to have cash to make a larger purchase. Cashing out on your equity is also used for paying off some types of debt such as credit card debt.

• Consolidate debt – loan refinancing is also used as a method to cope with increased level of debt(s) or variety of debt(s). Namely, you take one larger loan to refinance all outstanding debts. Meaning that you are consolidating the different types of debt(s).

While you should understand what it means to refinance a loan, it is also important for you to understand the reason behind the refinancing actions. Is your reason for refinancing mentioned in the above list?

Aside of the reasons for refinancing, try to think for a moment about the benefits and drawbacks of loan refinancing. Have you thought of any positive or negative side of refinancing?

Refinancing your mortgage has certain advantages for you as a borrower. Some of the common advantages are:

• Possibility to lower interest rate;
• Possibility to save money;
• Access to cash for larger purchases;
• Access to cash to pay off accumulated credit card debt;
• Lower monthly payment;
• Faster repayment of your loan (mortgage);

There are also some drawbacks when refinancing your mortgage or loans in general. You should be well aware about these pitfalls before making any final decision. Some drawbacks are:

- Costly penalties (fees) for early repayment of your mortgage;
- Additional fees such as fee for legal advise;
- You could end up with larger debt;

Regardless of the opinion of some people, refinancing your mortgage doesn't have to be a complicated process. In many cases it can be a straight forward process. Of course the ease depends on many things. Things such as your credit score can have influence on possibility to get approved. Moreover, choosing the wrong bank to refinance with, could result in complication of the refinancing process.

In simple terms, the general overview of the refinancing process is as follows:

1. Go through the agreement of your original mortgage – you should be aware about the terms and conditions of your original mortgage. Make sure that you understand the fees and additional charges you will have to pay in case you refinance. See if refinancing is worth the effort. Are you going to save money after you refinance? Try asking for an advice from professional.

2. Shop around for adequate loan – this step is crucial because you should carefully analyze the different offers and promotions available. Don't be lazy because there can be substantial differences from one offer to another, especially if it is about a mortgage loan. Try to find the best offer out there.

3. Choose your lender – basically you have two choices either to stay with the current lender or switch to a new bank. People usually go with the bank (or lender) offering better terms.

4. Applying for a refinance loan – this step is rather self-explanatory.

5. Approval and documentation – you should gather the necessary document and deliver them to your bank. The bank will go through the documentation and start processing the application. If you satisfy the lenders criteria, you should be informed.

6. Loan settlement – in this step title should be exchanged and the mortgage on your property is registered.

7. Well done – you have finished the refinancing process. If you have applied for a cash out refinancing, this is where you should see the cash on your hand.

You should not forget that refinancing your mortgage might turn out to be a costly process. You should understand the different fees you might have to pay if you want to refinance your mortgage or apply for a refinance loan. Some of these fees can be rather substantial amount of money as well. Consequently, common fees you might have to pay when refinancing are:

• Pre-payment penalty – is penalty for early repayment of your mortgage (or other loans for that matter). Basically, the existing lender will charge certain penalty because you are paying off the mortgage prior to the agreed maturity. Go through the agreement of your original mortgage and see if there is a penalty for early repayment.

• Application fee – serves the purpose to cover the cost of going through borrowers credit report check. The application fee charged by the lender is also covering the initial process costs of the loan. Application fee is usually up to $500.

• Appraisal fee – is fee associated with the house appraisal. Lenders require for a property appraisal in order to see if the value (and build up equity if needed) is sufficient for you to qualify for refinancing. The cost for appraising your house is usually from $300 to $500, but it can go higher or lower. On the basis of appraised value you can see whether it is smart move to refinance or not. If loan to value ratio is higher than 80% reconsider the need for new mortgage.

• Loan origination fee – is usually around 1% of the value of your loan.

• Documentation preparation fee – can be charged by some lenders, it can also be as high as $400 or more.

• Title search fee – is applied because the lender might need a title search. Commonly, this fee is around $200 to $500.

• Title insurance – to cover the potential loss of ownership interest in some property (as a result of legal problems) both the lender and the homeowner will expected the purchase of title insurance. Title insurance can cost from $400 to $800.

Going through the mortgage refinance costs you can see that the difference in interest rate is not the sole factor for deciding whether to refinance or not. There are numerous additional charges that you should pay when applying for a refinance loan. These additional fees come in the form of application costs, administration cost, appraisal costs and legal fees. All together these fees can amount to several thousands of dollars. Also, keep in mind that some lenders have hidden fees (don't work with these lenders).

Is mortgage refinancing for everybody?

Mortgage refinancing is specifically good for borrowers with high credit score. They could use the refinancing option in order to switch from variable interest mortgage to fixed interest rate mortgage. Refinancing is not recommended if you have lower credit score. But this doesn't mean that you shouldn't gather information to see if you'll be better off or worse off if you decide to refinance. Always gather information before making any decisions.

Mortgage refinancing could be for you in some specific circumstances. Namely, you could consider the refinancing option if for whatever reason you know that you will not be able to afford the monthly payment. If you have decrease in your income, you can try to refinance your loans as well. Although the first thing would be to discuss with your lender to modify the mortgage terms.

Types of refinancing

There are two commonly used types of refinancing: rate and term refinancing and cash-out refinancing. Rate and term refinancing is taking into consideration (as the name implies) interest rate and terms of existing mortgage.

Rate and term refinancing

Borrower who is applying for rate and terms refinancing wants to change the features of the existing mortgage.

Your new mortgage could be for a shorter term with a lower interest rate. For instance, your original mortgage is $200,000 for a 30-years period @5.8%. You will refinance your original mortgage with new mortgage of $200,000 for a 15-year period @ 4.25%. Noteworthy mentioning is that the interest rate can be either adjustable or fixed. Replacing your original mortgage with new mortgage with lower repayment period at lower interest rate.

This means that you are changing your old mortgage with a new one with better rate and term. This should eventually lead toward saving money on your mortgage.

Cash out refinancing

Aside of the desire to change terms and rate on your mortgage, the second method i.e. cash method is used exactly as it name implies. With the cash out method you basically want to refinance your original mortgage and get cash.

For instance, your original mortgage is $250,000 for a 30-years period @5.8% (adjustable or fixed interest rate). The cash out refinance mortgage would be $300,000 for a 30-years period @4.25%. After you pay off your original mortgage you will have $50,000 cash.

With cash out refinance you will replace your existing mortgage with larger mortgage. This way you are left with cash on hand after original mortgage is repaid. When using this form of refinancing, the homeowner is using the accumulated equity.

Negative side of cash out refinance is that you will be left with higher mortgage amount than the original one. Meaning that you will increase your debt.

Things to consider before refinancing

There are couple of basic things to consider before you decide to apply for loan refinancing. You should take into consideration your ability to qualify for a loan, your financial situation, reason why you want to refinance etc. In addition, try to use a mortgage refinance calculator so you would know approximately whether refinancing is worth the effort.

Ability to qualify for refinancing

It would be nice if you now beforehand whether or not you would qualify for a loan refinance. If possible, check whether the value of your home is lower than your loan amount. If it is lower, than it would be rather difficult (or very expensive) for you to qualify for a loan. Check if property value in your area has increased or decreased over the years. Don't rush into applying just to find out that you cannot qualify.

Assess you financial situation

If the value of your home is adequate, try to make assessment of your financial situation. The aim is for you to determine beforehand, your eligibility for a refinance loan. You should check for any items on your credit report which should be removed. If your credit score is lower try to improve it. Another thing your lender will take into consideration, is your debt to income ratio. Understand this ratio and the way it is calculated. Doing these couple of things might save you both time and money.

Shop around for adequate loan

Some people rush into things and apply for the first loan they see, only to find out later that another bank offered much better terms. Thus, you need to shop around for an adequate loan. Make sure that you know what would be an adequate loan for you. Compare the loans from different lenders in terms of costs, repayment term, monthly payments and fees.

Mortgage refinance calculator

Mortgage refinance calculator can be a practical tool to help you in the process of deciding whether or not to you should refinance you mortgage. Of course in order to use a mortgage refinance calculator you need to know couple of things. You should know the interest rate on your current and new mortgage, monthly payment, current loan amount, as well as the refinancing costs.

Loan refinancing can be a smart move when it comes to save money on your debt, especially your mortgage loan. Mortgage refinancing is offering the possibility for lowering your interest rate, lowering monthly payment, or paying off your debt faster. But also refinancing has its own drawbacks. If you misinterpret some factors, you could end up with costly refinancing, which will mean no savings.

Consequently, if you want to enjoy the benefits of refinancing, make sure that you understand what is loan refinancing. Second, understand the pros and cons of refinancing and the way this process works. Always try to gather sufficient information in order to make a wise decision. A decision which will help you to be in a good financial health.

4.5 Credit Card Balance Transfer Explained

Credit cards are a financial instrument followed by numerous advantages and disadvantages. Credit cards could offer many benefits if used properly, or be a reason for a headache if not used in a proper manner. For this reason, you should make a careful (informed) decision regarding the need for a credit card, and the manner in which you will use it.

It could be noted that one problem that could appear when having (and using) credit cards, is the level of debt. Namely, you might be faced with large outstanding balance and most probably being charged with high APR. Therefore, you need to find a way to either repay your debt or at least lower your interest cost. The best thing would be to do both if possible. One choice you have to lower your APR along with the possibility to repay your debt faster, is the credit card balance transfer. Hence, it is important that you have gathered information and understand what credit card balance transfer is and how it works.

Balance transfer defined

If you are using a credit card(s) there is a risk (danger) that you might accumulate high-interest debt. In addition, you might be faced with a multiple debt payments on multiple credits card, even if you are paying the minimum amount on your credit cards. Faced with this situation, you could start searching for a solution to your credit card debt problem. In general, you have couple of basic options, either repay the debt in full, try to decrease the interest cost or consolidate the multiple payments into one payment. While the first option imposes the need for you to have substantial amount, depending on your debts, the second could be executed using a credit card balance transfer.

For this reason, the first thing you should do is to understand what credit card balance transfer is. It represents a process of taking a new credit card with low (even zero APR sometimes) interest rate, for the purpose of paying off balances on existing credit cards (or loans). The paying off is performed by transferring the existing balances to your new credit card.

Things to know about balance transfer

Before going for the balance transfer credit card, there are things you should be aware off. Knowing these things would help you to better understand the credit card balance transfer. These are:

- Understand the difference between balance transfer and repaying – you might misinterpret the purpose of balance transfer. When you make a credit card balance transfer you are not becoming debt free. You simply transfer the existing balance, and continue paying monthly payments. The aim of doing this is to benefit from the lower APR, thus saving money.

- Consolidate multiple payments – is possible thanks to the balance transfer. Meaning that, in case you have more than one credit card, you will have multiple monthly payments. Keeping track of multiple payments across different credit cards can be time consuming and confusing. Thus, by making a balance transfer you will consolidate these multiple payments into one monthly payment.

- Balance transfer is not limited to credit card debt – although it is most commonly used for credit card debt, you can also use it for other debts. Namely, you can use balance transfer to consolidate loans used for different purchases (such as car, furniture, etc.). In general, it could be done for most monthly installment payments. The process is executed through checks issued by the bank (credit card issuer).

- Know the balance transfer fees – since nothing is given for free, neither is the balance transfer option. For this reason, you should always pay attention to possible fees you will be charged with. Make sure that you are informed about the balance transfer fee charged as a percentage of the total amount you want to transfer. Typical balance transfer fee could be around 3%. Meaning that, when calculating expected savings from balance transfer to low interest rate, you must add the transfer fees. Let's say that you want to transfer a $10,000 credit card debt, this means that you will pay $300 in balance transfer fee.

- The expiration date of low APR – do not forget that the new credit card with low APR has an expiration date. Stated differently the low APR offer is for a limited time, often around 12 months (it can be for longer or shorter period). After the predetermined period of low APR is over, the interest rate will drastically increase to more than 12% (depending on multiple factors). This is concerning you because, this APR is most probably higher than what you have paid on your old credit card. Thus, if you fail to pay your monthly obligations on time, and repay the balance owed (at least portion of it) during the APR promotional period, your initially planned savings will disappear.

- Control your shopping urges – don't get into the psychological trap of making new purchases just because you have a low or even a 0% APR balance transfer on your new credit card. Make sure that you go through the entire agreement carefully. This is because in some cases the low interest rate is only applicable to the balance transferred, and is not applicable to new purchases. Consequently, all new purchases bear higher APR. Make sure you know whether the low APR is applicable only to balance transferred or it can apply to new purchases.

• Get acquainted with the Credit CARD Act of 2009 – dedicating some time to go through the Act will help you better understand your rights as a consumer, not only in terms of balance transfer, but also for other credit card related issues. In accordance with the aforementioned Act it is required that: *a card issuer, upon receipt of payment, to apply amounts in excess of the minimum payment amount first to the balance bearing the highest rate of interest, and then to each successive balance bearing the next highest rate of interest, until the payment is exhausted* (Source – Public Law No: 111-24 (05/22/2009)). This means that you cannot influence the way your payments are disbursed if you have low interest balance transfer balance and new purchase balance with higher APR on the same credit card. For this reason, it might be wise not to use your new balance transfer credit card for purchases.

• Resist the temptation of repeating the process – avoid repeating the balance transfer process after the low APR period is over. Although it might seems to you that you could be riding the benefits from low APR continuously, don't do it. Repeating the balance transfer process could have negative impact on your credit score. Lenders might perceive you as a risky borrower because you are constantly retaining higher level of debt, although you are using the balance transfer.

• The importance of good credit score – in order to enjoy better terms on your balance transfer credit card, it is highly important for you to have high credit score. The higher your credit score, the better terms you will get from the lender. This means that you can even qualify for a 0% APR on your balance transfer. Keep in mind thought, that maxing out your credit card could influence your debt-to-income ratio.

Whatever anyone says, the final decision regarding the need to make a balance transfer, should and will be entirely yours. For this reason, you should gather as much information as possible, and understand all important aspects. Therefore, you should consider some of the advantages and disadvantages before making a balance transfer. Some of them are listed below:

Advantages of balance transfer

• Save money on your interest rate – lower interest means that your debt is much cheaper, thus the lower the interest the more you save on your outstanding balance.

• Consolidate multiple payments into one – this will drastically simplify your finances and make your life easier.

• Pay off your debt faster – because you are paying lower (even 0%) APR for a certain period, it means that you could be making larger payment toward the principal amount. Meaning that, the money you are saving could be directed toward repayment of the outstanding balance, above the minimum payment required by the credit. This way you are able to repay your debt much faster. This is a benefit only if your financial situation allows you to redirect your savings towards balance repayment.

Disadvantages of balance transfer

• You will pay a balance transfer fee – this fee could eat up portion of your savings. Therefore, make sure you understand all fees and possible savings associated with the balance transfer. Do not end up making the balance transfer, while fees are eating up your savings.

• Effect on credit score – balance transfer could have a small negative effect on your credit score in the short run.

• Higher interest rate after low interest rate period is over – most probably your new credit card will charge you a higher interest rate after the period is over. Thus, not repaying your debt during the low interest rate period, will result in increased cost on your outstanding balance.

Whatever decision you are making in relation to your finances and financial products, always consider the advantages and disadvantages. This can be a strategy which will help you to easily understand all possible benefits, as well as the things you could lose.

How to choose adequate balance transfer offer?

Although each and every one of us might have different needs when it comes to a financial matters, we still search for some common features when it comes to balance transfer. Thus, you should make sure that you have considered all available options before choosing the balance transfer offer. Consequently, in order to get the most out of your balance transfer, you should pay attention to the following:

• Search for an offer with 0% APR, and no balance transfer fee.

• If multiple offers fulfill the aforementioned criteria, then look for the period of the offer. The longer the period of 0% APR the more you save.

• Make sure that you understand how much you will save, and accordingly calculate your possible savings. See how balance transfer fee will influence your savings level.

• Make an effort to repay your debt before the low interest rate period is over.

• You will have to decide what you want to do with your old credit card account. If you keep your old account open you could be charging small amount (gas bill for instance) every month or so and paying off this balance in full. This could have positive impact on your credit score. On the other hand, it could lead toward increase in your debt levels, if you start using your old credit card on regular bases for larger purchases.

• Make regular payments, missing a payment could result in termination of the low interest rate agreement. Afterwards, you will be stacked with paying a regular interest rate.

• It was previously mentioned that you can increase your score by charging small amounts on your old credit card. If you start making larger purchases with the old credit card, then you will be in worse position, since you have accumulated additional debt.

It is obvious by now that a balance transfer has the potential to save you a substantial amount of money. That is, if it is executed in the right manner. Therefore, the first thing you should do before making a balance transfer, you must read the agreement of your existing credit card, and get acquainted with the terms of the deal. Next, although interest rate is highly important, other aspects of the new credit card deal should be considered before making any final decision.

Balance transfer example

After explaining what balance transfer is, it is time to see an illustrative example about the benefits one might have from balance transfer. Before going to the example, it should be pointed out that this is an illustrative example. If you are planning to make a balance transfer, ask from the bank (your new credit card issuer) to give you exact calculations. This way you will have the information applicable to your financial situation.

Let's consider a person who has a current balance of $7,000 being charged with 16% APR. In accordance to the current terms, if a fixed payment of $300 is made each billing cycle, it would take 29 monthly payments for the balance to be repaid. The interest charge would be approximately $1,440.

Now imagine that there is a credit card balance transfer offer with 0% APR for 15 months (the 0% applies for the first 15 months). It should be noted that there are offers where the 0% APR period could be more than 15 months. After the low interest rate period is over, the regular APR is 17%. There is also a 3% balance transfer fee. Under the assumption that the monthly payment is fixed at $300 each month, it will take 24 months for the balance to be repaid. This is five months less until the debt is paid off compared to the current situation. In addition, by paying off the balance in 24 monthly (where the first 15 months are with 0% APR) the interest saved would be a bit more than a $1,000. This saving is after the balance transfer fee of $210 is paid. Keep in mind that the best thing would be if you could repay the full outstanding balance within the low interest rate period.

How would you feel if you could save hundreds if not thousands of dollars in interest charge? How would you feel if you have the possibility to pay off your credit card debt months even years earlier? Before applying for a credit card balance transfer, shop around for an adequate offer – You can find balance transfer credit cards examples as well as offers easily online.

4.6 Conclusion

One of the most important aspects of personal finance is the need for adequate debt management practices. Defining an adequate strategy for managing your debt imposes the need for better understanding of the basics concepts and methods for coping with debt.

When talking about the debt repayment, it should be noted that a borrower might either be overindebted and must find a way to repay the debt or simply the borrower may want to pay off the debt faster. Although there are some overlapping strategies for both situations, being overindebted requires extra efforts for the purpose of coping with the debt.

Loan refinancing is commonly used strategy when it comes to debt management. Loan refinancing offers numerous benefits for the borrower. In addition, credit card balance transfer is viable option for dealing with credit card debt. This form of debt is one of the most expensive debt we could have. Thus, the balance transfer credit card offers the possibility for decrease in the cost of credit card debt as long as the terms of this repayment method are fulfilled.

ABOUT THE AUTHOR

Zoran Temelkov, Assistant Professor at University "Goce Delcev", Shtip, Macedonia.